SANTA MONICA PIER

America's Last Great Pleasure Pier

SANTA MONICA
PIER

America's Last
Great Pleasure Pier

James Harris

foreword by Robert Redford

afterword by Arnold Schwarzenegger

This book is dedicated to everyone who ever loved the Santa Monica Pier.

Contents

Santa Monica, Cal.

Foreword

As I reflect upon Santa Monica Pier—a place of significant personal experience and great history, I am struck by the importance it plays on an individual level, in the community, and as an internationally recognized symbol of California. When I was a child, it was the wild frontier—the escape from the city to the east. It was a place of vision and creativity where I spent hours enjoying the rides and games, marveling at the skill of the fishermen, and enjoying the ocean air, wide-open skies and endless horizon.

My folks and I lived in a lower-working-class neighborhood in Santa Monica, and there wasn't much to do except go to the ocean, walk the boardwalk, build castles in the sand and imagine magical things. It was Santa Monica Pier that revealed to me I was four years old. I was walking with my grandmother along the boardwalk when another kid accosted me. He asked me how old I was and I must have said four, because he laughed and said, "Well, I'm five. I'm older than you." I remember his hat (a sailor hat), behind him the merry-go-round on the pier circling and circling, and the uneven sound of the calliope's music, fresh and tantalizing. That was one of my first memories of childhood, and it burned its image in my mind forever.

Since 1909 the pier has remained a constant of the Southern California coastline and has weathered many storms, enduring lean economic times and the power of Mother Nature. L.A. has served up many of its historic landmarks to the ugly ravages of development and progress. As such, in 1973, Santa Monica

Santa Monica Municipal Pier and Looff Pleasure Pier, 1917.

Pier was slated for demolition, set to follow Venice Pier and Pacific Ocean Park Pier into memory and lore.

The filming of *The Sting* coincided with this pivotal moment in pier history. As we used the inherent historic qualities of the carousel to recreate 1930s Chicago for the movie, we became acutely aware of the importance of the effort to preserve the pier's actual history. This film location had also been a scene of joy in my own life years earlier. The real and "reel" worlds joined together in that time and space… at least for me (and that is just one story of so many that have taken place for each and every person who has visited the pier over the last hundred years).

It was an important experience for me, and a pivotal moment for the fate of the pier as well. I was impressed by the power of community activism that had developed, and it was with pride that I joined so many others in signing the petition to save the structure and its many facets.

The knowledge that our creative filmmaking efforts on the pier played a role in the preservation of the physical historic landmark serves as a lasting testament to the power of the pier as a place that marries lore, fact, fiction, dreams, reality and the power of a grassroots movement to preserve this treasure for all to enjoy. Walking on the pier, one can simultaneously experience the fantastic reality of the wind, waves, sand, and creaking wooden decks, and travel back in time to the simple pleasures of the carousel and its timeless amusement.

I have had the great fortune of viewing the pier through several sets of eyes—those of a child, an adult, a professional, and an old friend. As you peruse the pages of this book, I hope that you too enjoy the journey of cherished youth, triumph over adversity and challenge, and growth from modest beginnings to becoming an icon. The pier reminds me of our youth, our innocence. Such places are hard to find.

Welcome to *Santa Monica Pier, America's Last Great Pleasure Pier.*

—Robert Redford

Introduction

The Santa Monica Pier is one of the most recognizable landmarks in Southern California, and perhaps even the world. For well over a century, the pier has successfully withstood many dramatic tests: of changes of culture and purpose, of threats presented by Mother Nature, of its own perception and popularity, and of time. It has created memories and carried meaning for uncountable numbers of people throughout its existence, and it boasts a most fascinating story of growth from humble beginnings into an icon recognized worldwide.

When the pier opened as a modest, narrow, and overall unimpressive structure in the early twentieth century, it was nevertheless welcomed by thousands of visitors. It was a favorite among the fishing community, it had a sense of purpose, and it was 100 percent Santa Monica's pier. Today, it is completely different. It is complex, it is wide, and its wide variety of offerings can cause one's head to spin. And yet today it remains what it once was, what it has always been. It is beloved by the fishing community, it is endowed with great purpose, and it is still 100 percent Santa Monica's pier.

In the grand collection of pleasure piers throughout the world, the Santa Monica Pier has emerged as arguably the most recognized pier in the world. The United Kingdom has its great pier—the granddaddy of all amusement park piers—in the Brighton Palace Pier, and Chicago's Navy Pier is the largest pier in the world. The Santa Monica Pier makes no claim as the oldest or the largest. In fact, throughout the history of piers, the Santa Monica Pier couldn't even claim one of those titles amongst its nearby sister piers in the Santa Monica Bay, such as Abbot Kinney's Venice Pier or the short-lived but beloved Pacific Ocean Park pier (POP), most of which disappeared long ago. But the Santa Monica Pier has its very own unique claim to greatness, built upon its longevity, its ingenuity of reinvention and, most important of all, its effect upon people. The Santa Monica Pier has had such a profound

impact that it is impossible to even imagine Santa Monica—or even the greater Los Angeles area—without the four-acre structure that has been the one true constant that people everywhere recognize.

When the first edition of this book was published, the prevailing atmosphere in Santa Monica was that the pier had finally found itself. It had withstood one hundred years of trials, tribulations, and tests to its very existence. After near-demolition, first by man, then by nature, it was restored and reimagined to become something worthy of the appreciation that saved it—twice. In hindsight, the value of the great structure was always there, hidden in its history that was told both in that first edition of this book, and then in the tales that have been unveiled since. There is an important story in every part of the pier, at every corner, within every deck board, and, while each specific story is perhaps relevant to only a certain few people, the stories are numerous enough to strike meaning with everyone. Beach culture has deep roots here, as does pop culture, and so much of what Southern California is recognized for. So many things began here—*literally began here!* The cultural impact of the Santa Monica Pier is felt not just on the city or the Los Angeles region, but on the entire world.

While the Santa Monica Pier is not the oldest pleasure pier, nor the largest, nor even the most distinct in its own neighborhood's history, it is the pier that best symbolizes pier and beach culture. That honor was earned through the delicate combination of factors contributed by the very special people who have been a part of its history. There is something about the Santa Monica Pier that has somehow managed to welcome people's ideas, concepts, and ingenuity. The pier has touched the soul of every person who has visited it and reciprocally been touched in kind. And that, I believe, is what gives the pier its enduring meaning and value, making the Santa Monica Pier what it is today—the last great pleasure pier.

Fishermen on the pier, 1930s.

The profile of the Santa Monica Pier, seen here in 1917, has evolved over a century but is still instantly recognizable in any era.

1

THE WEST COAST'S FIRST CONCRETE PIER

*O*rgan music emanates from the carousel building while, inside, hand-carved wooden horses race in an endless circle. Laughter resonates through the air as wooden deck boards creak beneath people's footsteps, the rhythmic roar of the waves never far away. A cool breeze carries the aroma of hamburgers, broiled fish, and fresh-popped popcorn, all mixing splendidly with the salt air. A roller coaster thunders along its track as passengers scream with delight. Seagulls chatter above erratic rows of fishing poles propped up along the blue railing, joining in the hope for a successful day's catch. Dancing lights invite passersby to board the Ferris wheel…

Who can imagine this pier as anything less than a fanciful getaway? However, its original purpose was far from magical—it was born as a simple public utility. The growth of Santa Monica in the early twentieth century forced the

Commemorative medallions were distributed to attendees of the opening ceremony of the Santa Monica Municipal Pier. Opposite: Postcard depicting opening day, September 9, 1909.

city to confront a very serious sewage disposal problem. After considering several options, officials agreed that the best method was to cast the sewage out to sea. But since Santa Monica was already so well known for its beautiful, clean beaches, the notion of polluting the community's own water was preposterous. Careful studies, however, concluded that a pier could carry the waste far enough past the surf that it would wash out to sea, not back to the shore. Property interests in the Colorado Avenue area allowed the city to use their land, and the city immediately proceeded to build a long pier.

L.G. Osgood of the California Ornamental Brick Company recommended using concrete to construct the pier. Wooden piers were notorious victims both of the weather and of infestation by wood-burrowing clams called shipworms or Teredo worms. Osgood pointed out the successful use of concrete piers in Europe and in Atlantic City, New Jersey. The city council concurred, making it the first concrete pier on the West Coast. On September 28, 1907, the public voted in favor of a $150,000 bond to build the proposed pier.

Of eleven plans submitted for the new pier, the city council chose local architect Edwin H. Warner's design,

which proposed a 1,600-foot-long pier supporting an eighteen-inch outfall pipe running underneath the entire length of the pier's floor, inclined so that gravity would carry the treated waste to the ocean. The plan included a treatment plant on the beach at the foot of the pier, designed to purify the sewage and pump it into the outfall pipe for disposal.

The construction contract was awarded to the Stutzer Cement and Grading Company under the supervision of Santa Monica City Engineer Thomas James. On April 8, 1908, work began with casting the concrete piles. Materials were readily available, for there was certainly ample sand for the concrete mix. Pile driving began in May 1908, and construction progressed rapidly, at the rate of four piles per day. Journalists arrived from across the country to observe the construction of the West Coast's unique new concrete pier, and in turn became well acquainted with the charming seaside community where it stood.

Left: Concrete piles curing before installation of the new pier. Right: Early stage of construction, 1909

Santa Monica was abuzz over potential activities and enterprises that the pier could accommodate. Proposals ranged from a simple bandstand to a highly ambitious yacht harbor. The city council, also recognizing the potential, yet concerned over growing frustrations with local alcohol use, passed an ordinance outlawing the distribution of liquor on the new pier. Regardless, the members reasoned, the new pier was bound to become an inviting new destination.

On August 18, 1909, after sixteen months of construction, the new pier was completed with only a few minor finishing details remaining, and Mayor T.H. Dudley declared September 9—the anniversary of California's statehood—the official opening day of the new Santa Monica Municipal Pier.

Thousands of people from all over Southern California attended the grand opening and dedication ceremony, a full day of festivities and activities commemorating

the city's magnum opus—the West Coast's first concrete pier. The celebration commenced with a parade that began at Santa Monica City Hall and ended at the foot of the new pier, where Mayor Dudley dedicated it and the featured speaker, State Senator Lee C. Gates commended the citizens of Santa Monica for their energy, spirit, and courage for using groundbreaking technology. Santa Monica, he declared, had set the precedent for all future piers.

The celebration progressed throughout the day with swimming, running, and boating competitions. George Freeth, one of Southern California's first lifeguards and recognized as "The Father of Modern Surfing," was among the judges for the day's contests. The naval cruiser USS *Albany* and her accompanying flotilla dropped anchor off the end of the pier to honor the celebration as crowds gathered to view the great vessels up close. That night, a band concert continued the celebration, and a *tableau vivant* entitled *The Surrender of Rex Neptune* brought the party to a climax. The theatrical production portrayed a battle of wits between the notorious sea lord Rex Neptune and Queen Santa Monica, whose new concrete pier was strong enough to withstand any of Neptune's legendary storms. Fireworks highlighted the defeated Neptune's fiery descent back into the sea.

Left: Construction workers prepare a concrete pile to be driven into the ocean floor using jet-propulsion of water through a pipe down the center of the pile. Right: The underside of the completed Municipal Pier.

The new Municipal Pier begins to take shape, mid-1909.

It didn't take long for the Municipal Pier to find its most exuberant and loyal fans: the fishing community. The first fish caught on the pier was landed by John McCreery on August 30, 1909—a full week before the pier officially opened. The new pier was instantly touted as the best fishing spot on Santa Monica Bay.

During the decade that followed, the Municipal Pier remained a popular destination. Neighboring amusement piers may have been flashier and more alluring, but the Municipal Pier remained distinctly original. The "indestructible" new technology, however, proved less than its billing. On August 17, 1919, a sizable crowd, including Mayor Samuel L. Berkley, gathered at the west end of the pier for passage to tour the battleship USS *Texas* and cruiser USS *Prairie*, both anchored in the bay. Suddenly, a twenty-foot section on the north-end side of the pier shook, groaned, and then dropped approximately two feet toward the ocean. Although no one was hurt, the city closed the pier immediately.

Four children, including two grandsons of Santa Monica co-founder Senator John P. Jones, enjoy a visit to the new Santa Monica Municipal Pier, c. 1920

The Surrender of Neptune A Tableau Vivant

September 9, 1909. The great Rex Neptune climbed upon the newly built pier in Santa Monica, California, determined to demonstrate his command over the sea and all those who trespass upon it. Queen Santa Monica, undaunted by the great sea lord's ominous presence, inquired why he would dare interrupt this glorious public gathering. He had the reputation, after all, of destroying so many prized piers throughout his storied career. Neptune casually replied that destroying piers simply amused him, and that he would take special delight in destroying this new, unusual looking structure. The Queen scoffed at him, announcing that this pier was made of concrete—impossible even for him to destroy. Neptune surveyed the strong stone-like structure, humbly turned toward the Queen and admitted defeat. The Queen ordered him back to his ocean home, never to return to this indestructible pier, and Rex Neptune dove off the pier covered in a blaze of flames.

Officials initially blamed the incident on drifting wreckage from the Long Wharf, once a mile-long pier a few miles north, which had inflicted damage two years earlier. Inspection by commissioned engineers, however, revealed that most of the venerable concrete pilings were on the verge of collapse due to rust and disintegration. Further inspection showed that fewer than ten percent of the pilings were sound. The engineers determined that the beach sand used in the initial composition of the concrete was too porous and permeable, compromising the structural integrity of the piles. After careful consideration, City Commissioner William H. Carter recommended that the most suitable replacement would be cre-

osote-treated wooden piles and substructure. Treated piles were believed to be equally long-lasting and certainly less expensive than concrete.

A $75,000 bond issue was placed upon the ballot with strong support from Mayor Berkley. The *Evening Outlook* added its support as well, expressing its opinion on the matter in no uncertain terms: SHOULD DISASTER COME TO THE MUNICIPAL PIER...SEWAGE

Opening day of the Municipal Pier featured a parade from city hall and speeches by Santa Monica Mayor T.H. Dudley and California State Senator Lee C. Gates.

Thousands of people walked the 1,600-foot-long pier on its opening day, while a United States Navy flotilla anchored just beyond the pier's end.

WOULD FLOW DIRECTLY INTO THE OCEAN ON OUR IMMEDIATE SHORES AND DISEASE AND DEATH WOULD SURELY FOLLOW IT.

The bond passed by a two-thirds majority on January 1, 1920. Replacement of the concrete piles commenced almost three months later. Holes were cut into the concrete floor of the pier through which new wooden piles were driven. The holes were subsequently patched with new concrete. The process, so novel that *Popular Mechanics* magazine featured it, was completed on November 17, under budget by $15,000.

The Municipal Pier reopened to the public in January 1921, a little less remarkable than it had been. Then, in 1928, the Municipal Pier lost its distinction as a public utility when Santa Monica joined neighboring Los Angeles and Venice in a new sewage disposal project that transported the west side's waste south to the new Hyperion sewage treatment plant in El Segundo. Finally, in the early 1930s, even the concrete deck was replaced with wooden planks. Yet while the Municipal Pier was no longer the marvel so heralded in 1909, it survived as a magnet for fishermen, sea lovers, and entrepreneurs.

Opening day visitors enjoyed a full day of activities that included athletic competitions on the beach, a *tableau vivant* performance, and an evening fireworks show.

Sea Monsters Fictional & Factual

What would a seaside community be without a good sea monster story? The first recorded sighting near the pier occurred in September of 1888: a creature resembling a giant black snake was reported about a mile-and-a-half north of Municipal Pier's site. A more detailed and humorous sighting came in June 1917 as the story of the "Sea Serpent of Santa Monica Pier" took the police, the press and the town by storm:

> Sea Serpent Off City Pier
> S-s-s-h!
> It was early.
> The sea serpent was with us.
> It was the real sea serpent, with his flowing mane of green locks. His massive head and trailing body wound in undulating lengths behind him. There was still a little of the darkness of the night before left over, so that the fire the serpent blew from his snake shaped mouth could be seen. His snakeship, according to the one man and then the other three men, was moving from the north to the south. The more morning broke, the greater in size became the sea serpent. As it increased in size, the mammoth head and neck became elevated and began to sway gently from side to side. The tale of what the three men saw was soon being told of as a fact along the oceanfront. It spread to Venice and was told of in Ocean Park. This telephone message was sent to the Santa Monica Police Headquarters: "Reported that a large sea serpent was seen off of the Municipal Pier early this morning." This telephone message was received at the Outlook office from Playa del Rey: "Great long string of kelp washed up on beach here. It is believed to have gotten away from the kelp cutters."

(Condensed excerpt from the *Santa Monica Evening Outlook*; June 28, 1917)

Many decades later, on February 24, 2012, Santa Monica City Painter Wayne von der Mehden was doing some touch up work on the railing at the west end of the pier when he noticed a commotion among a group of fishermen nearby. One of their fishing lines had just hooked something very large, perhaps a pesky sea lion. As the angler exercised his expertise by adjusting the drag on his line, the line snapped. According to von der Mehden, the angler's eyes widened as he realized that his lost catch was not a sea lion, but a humpback whale! Warmer ocean waters that winter encouraged whales to swim closer to shore during winter migration, with water spouts from whales becoming a frequent sight for viewers from the shore. Four years later, ironically on that same February 24 date, street performer Terry Prince captured on video a humpback whale breaching just beyond the pier's west end.

Carousel Park, located at the easternmost end of the pier, is a tribute to the legendary tales of when sea monsters ruled the ocean.

2

BIRTH OF THE AMUSEMENT PIER

*I*n the early part of the twentieth century, a multitude of seaside amusement piers in the Ocean Park and Venice areas beckoned hordes of people to the beach, adding to the allure of Santa Monica Bay. Ever since the completion of the Municipal Pier, Santa Monica's north beach community yearned to have its own amusement pier, and the most suitable location would be adjacent to the existing concrete pier.

At the time, the properties next to the Municipal Pier were owned by Carl F. Schader to the north and Edwin P. Benjamin and B. N. Moss to the south. Benjamin and Moss were first to act. On December 4, 1915, the pair applied to the United States Engineer with a request to build a seven-hundred-foot amusement pier on their property. Two months later, having received approval, Benjamin announced that the company had sold

Charles Looff said accessibility was a primary reason to build a pleasure pier adjacent to the Municipal Pier. Opposite: The completed Looff Pleasure Pier attached seamlessly to the Municipal Pier, creating the early foundation of what is known today as the Santa Monica Pier.

Nighttime view from the north of the brilliantly lit Santa Monica Pleasure Pier, featuring the Whirlwind Dipper roller coaster and palatial La Monica Ballroom, circa 1924.

the property to Charles I.D. Looff, a nationally known and respected amusement park entrepreneur ideally suited to completing the proposed venture. The citizens of Santa Monica lauded the announcement and welcomed Looff to the community.

Looff's fame as an amusement entrepreneur found its seeds in New York City some forty years earlier. Born in Denmark, Looff immigrated to the United States in 1870, then trained and found employment as a furniture carver. Aspiring to a more creative use for his talent, he began carving wooden animals and, in 1876, at the age of twenty-four, built an all-wooden carousel and installed it at Balmer's Bathing Pavilion at Coney Island. It was the first carousel at the legendary amusement area. Looff continued with a career in manufacturing carousels and other amusement rides, and, in the early 1900s, moved to Long Beach to tackle the growing West Coast market. After purchasing the property south of the Municipal Pier, he engaged his two sons, William and Arthur, to run the project. Arthur, a trained engineer, supervised all construction; William oversaw more intricate details, such as electricity and lighting.

Benjamin and Moss further developed the remainder of their property, adding a team of electric tramcars de-signed to traverse the promenade along the beachfront and to carry passengers from Red Line terminals at Hill and Main Streets in Los Angeles. They convinced Pacific Electric to establish an Air Line train terminal at the foot of the Looff Pier property. The popular Air Line was, at that time, the only train that took its passengers directly to the beaches, and the proposed location of the terminal greatly influenced Looff's decision to build in Santa Monica.

Construction on the new pier proceeded quickly. In the meantime, Charles Looff negotiated with the city for a proposed twenty-year franchise for the new pier and announced his intention to attach his amusement pier to the Municipal Pier, enabling easy access between the two. The Santa Monica Planning Commission approved the concept, and, after much debate, the Looff proposal was finally accepted, with the caveats that the city be fairly compensated and that an anti-liquor clause be added to

Left: A colorized postcard of the Looff Pleasure Pier and Santa Monica Municipal Pier. Right: Charles Looff, a famous carousel carver who became an amusement park entrepreneur. Opposite: Two of the Looff Pleasure Pier's featured attractions: "The Whip" thrill ride and the "What Is It" fun house, 1917.

BIRTH OF THE AMUSEMENT PIER

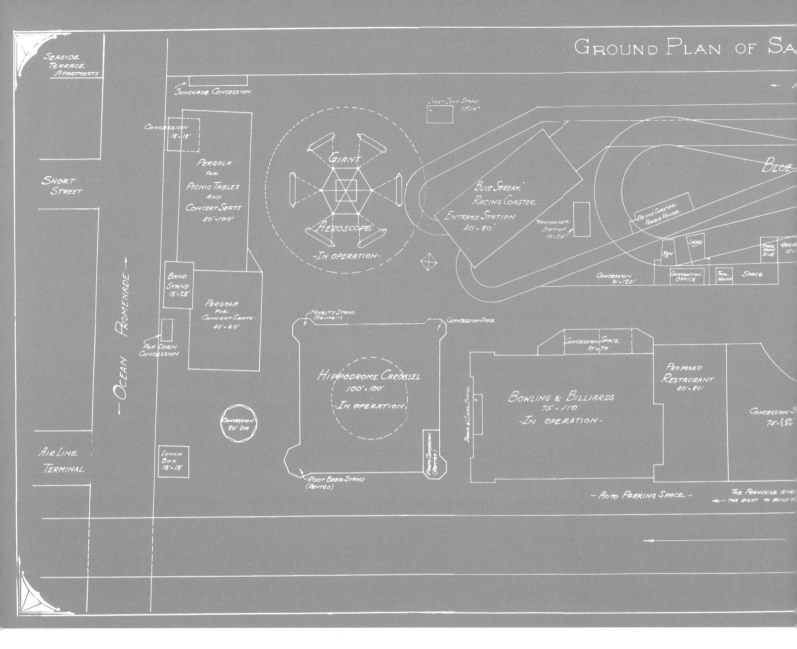

SEASIDE
TERRACE
APARTMENTS

SUNSHADE CONCESSION

SHORT
STREET

CONCESSION
18'×18'

PERGOLA
FOR
PICNIC TABLES
AND
CONCERT SEATS
40'×100'

SHEET-JEAN STAND
10'×14'

GIANT
AEROSCOPE
-IN OPERATION-

BLUE STREAK
RACING COASTER
ENTRANCE STATION
40'×80'

RACING COASTER
POWER HOUSE

BLUE

TRANSFORMER
STATION
10'×24'

MEN

LADIES

STORE
ROOM
10'×15'

GARA
15'

OCEAN PROMENADE

BAND
STAND
18'×28'

PERGOLA
FOR
CONCERT SEATS
40'×60'

POP CORN
CONCESSION

NOVELTY STAND
(RENTED)

CONCESSION SPACE

CONCESSION
18'×120'

CONSTRUCTION
OFFICE

TOOL
HOUSE

SPACE

CONCESSION SPACE
18'×70'

PROPOSED
RESTAURANT
40'×80'

CONCESSION S
75'×{59'

HIPPODROME CAROSSEL
100'×100'
-IN OPERATION-

CONCESSION
20' DIA

AIR LINE
TERMINAL

LUNCH
BOX
18'×18'

SODA & CIGAR STAND

POWER SHOW ROOM
(RENTED)

BOWLING & BILLIARDS
75'×110'
-IN OPERATION-

ROOT BEER STAND
(RENTED)

-AUTO PARKING SPACE-

THE FRANCHISE GIVE
THE RIGHT TO BUILD O

the agreement, since the pier had always been dry. The Looffs agreed, and the franchise was formally sold to them on June 1, 1916.

The new pier began to take shape in early June. The framework for the pier's roller coaster became visible and the carousel building, named the Looff Hippodrome, was nearly complete. The Hippodrome got its unusual name from the Greeks—"hippodrome" is Greek

for "horse racecourse." Wooden animals lined up inside the building, waiting to be mounted on the circular platform. On June 12, 1916, the carousel opened temporarily for a weekend, drawing people from all over Santa Monica. The following Fourth of July weekend was so busy that the still-unfinished Looff Pleasure Pier was clearly going to be the most popular pleasure pier on the entire West Coast.

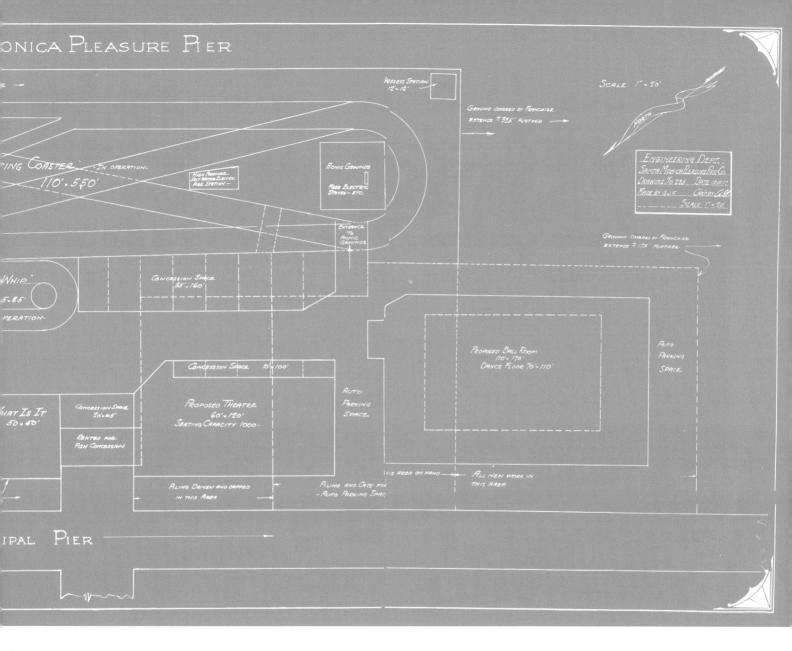

ONICA PLEASURE PIER

WRELESS STATION
12'×12'

GROUND COVERED BY FRANCHISE
EXTENDS ±375' FURTHER →

SCALE 1"=20'

NORTH

ENGINEERING DEPT.
SANTA MONICA PLEASURE PIER CO.
DRAWING No 235   DATE 1916/17
MADE BY G.J.F.   CHKD BY U.B
SCALE 1"=20'

ING COASTER   — IN OPERATION.
110'·550'

HIGH PRESSURE
SALT WATER ELECTRIC
FIRE STATION —

PICNIC GROUNDS

FREE ELECTRIC
STOVES — ETC.

GROUND COVERED BY FRANCHISE
EXTENDS ±175' FURTHER

WHIP"
5·85'
PERATION-

CONCESSION SPACE
35'·160'

ENTRANCE
TO
PICNIC
GROUNDS

PROPOSED BALL ROOM
110'·170'
DANCE FLOOR 70'·110'

AUTO
PARKING
SPACE

CONCESSION SPACE   10'·100'

HAT IS IT
50·50'

CONCESSION SPACE
20'·45'

RENTED FOR
FISH CONCESSION

PROPOSED THEATRE
60'·120'
SEATING CAPACITY 1000

AUTO
PARKING
SPACE

THIS AREA ON HAND   ALL NEW WORK IN
THIS AREA

PILING DRIVEN AND CAPPED
IN THIS AREA

PILING AND CAPS FOR
- AUTO PARKING SPACE

IPAL PIER

On August 3, 1916, the first screams were heard accompanying the roar of wheels speeding along the tracks of the Blue Streak Racer, the new roller coaster on the Looff Pleasure Pier. The screamers were carpenters and laborers who worked hard to construct the pier—that first ride was their reward. The following day, the coaster opened to the public, and the city held a grand opening ceremony to congratulate the Looffs for their efforts.

The Looff Pleasure Pier plans included a roller coaster, thrill rides, a carousel, and a bowling and billiards hall, all of which were in full swing by 1917. Plans for a theater and ballroom were also included, but never completed during the Looff family's ownership.

The new amusement pier included a picnic area at the foot of the coaster, complete with electric ovens. This picnic area was but a prelude, the Looffs announced, to a full-scale picnic pavilion planned for the pier's eastern end. More thrill rides were on tap; the Whip and the Aeroscope each opened within a month. In January 1917, the Bowling & Billiards Building opened, and its alleys and tables were an immediate success. In the spring, the anxiously awaited fun house, named "What Is It?", opened its doors. Inside, patrons walked through several levels of sight-and-balance gags such as shifting stairs and moving floors, culminating in a seventy-foot slide.

As promised, the new picnic pavilion was ready by late May. Picnic tables were arranged under a wooden canopy covered with palm leaves to provide shaded dining. The nearby bandstand was an ideal venue for weekend concerts. Professor Cesare La Monaca and his Royal Italian Band, one of the most popular bands on the Pacific Coast at the time, headlined at the Looff Pavilion on June 2, 1917, and performed as many as three shows a day. The Santa Monica Municipal Band later divided its time between the Looff Pleasure Pier and Ocean Park.

In December of 1917, Charles Looff sold stock in his new firm, the Santa Monica Pleasure Pier Company.

The stock initially sold well, and expansion quickly began. A two-story banquet hall went up just west of the Bowling & Billiards Building, and was ready March 15, 1918, in time to host its first of many groups, the Christian Endeavor Convention.

The Looff Pleasure Pier thrived during its first couple of years and plans were developed for continued expansion of its amusements, including an extension of the pier to accommodate a large ballroom. After Charles Looff's death in the summer of 1918, however, the optimism surrounding the pier began to fade. The company's stock collapsed; controversy over the Municipal Band splitting time between the Looff Pier and Ocean Park jeopardized concerts altogether, and Arthur Looff ultimately began spending the better part of his time and energy developing amusements for the Santa Cruz Beach

A large crowd of people gathers at the picnic pavilion and bandstand, just east of the Looff Hippodrome, while the Aeroscope thrills riders in the background. Opposite: The pier's first roller coaster, the Blue Streak Racer, debuted in August 1916.

Professor Cesare La Monaca and his Royal Italian Band. La Monaca was known not only for his musical prowess but also for his extensive collection of band uniforms.

An electric tram passes in front of the Looff Pleasure Pier, 1917.

Boardwalk. In January 1921, rumors circulated about the sale of the amusement pier. On September 14, 1923, it became official—the Looff Pier was sold to the Santa Monica Amusement Company, a syndicate composed of prominent local real-estate investors Edward B. Conliss, C.D. Terry, David D. Pascoe, and Dr. Frank J. Wagner.

The first priority for the Santa Monica Amusement Company was the replacement of the aging Blue Streak Racer. The firm hired the Whirlwind Dipper Company to construct a new roller coaster designed by the Prior & Church Company, owners of many of the rides in Venice and Ocean Park. Construction went quickly, and the new Whirlwind Dipper coaster opened its gates on March 30, 1924.

With the new coaster fully operational and successfully drawing people to the pier, the company turned its attention to its next great enterprise—the La Monica Ballroom. The plans were drawn by the internationally renowned architect T.H. Eslick, who had achieved an impeccable reputation, designing grand ballrooms in the United States, Europe, and Australia. Construction on the gigantic structure moved at an accelerated pace, with the La Monica scheduled to open in the early summer. Newspapers in both Santa Monica and Los Angeles steadily monitored its progress. On July 23, 1924, more than fifty thousand people arrived to witness the opening of the La Monica Ballroom, a crowd so immense that the event has since been credited with causing Santa Monica's first traffic jam. The La Monica was considered the most impressive structure of its kind, and became an instant success.

By 1925, though, business on all of the Santa Monica Bay's piers began to wane, a phenomenon credited to the recent availability of inexpensive used automobiles. Worsening matters for the Santa Monica Amusement Company, a storm rocked the pier and the La Monica, causing significant damage to the substructure and forcing the ballroom to close for repair. After the ballroom recovered, the Whirlwind Dipper faced near-disaster when a nineteen-year-old woman leaped off while it was nearing the end of a run. Admitting that she had been drinking with a few companions, the girl was lucky to suffer only a broken arm, some internal injuries, and cuts and bruises. The publicity did not help an already struggling operation, however. On September 1, 1927, Conliss, Terry, and Pascoe of the Santa Monica Amusement Company sold all of their interests to a newly formed syndicate, the Santa Monica Pier Amusement Company, headed by continuing owner Dr. Frank J. Wagner.

Among Dr. Wagner's first actions was the construction of a 150-foot extension to the southwest corner of the pier, just beyond the ballroom. The extended section was built in order to accommodate a new tenant, the Santa Monica Yacht and Motorboat Club, and resembled a third pier.

In late May of 1928, Dr. Wagner leased his entire concession rights to the Laumauro Amusement Company of New York. The new lessee invested one million dollars (more than eighteen million in 2023 dollars) into the creation of a theme park called "The City of Baghdad." The

View of the Looff Pleasure Pier and Municipal Pier from atop Santa Monica's northern palisades, 1917.

park was extensively redecorated to reflect the atmosphere of the old Eastern world and opened on June 30, 1928. Merchants in "The City of Baghdad" wore Arabian dress and, for ambience, a minstrel played Eastern music. An Eli 24 Ferris wheel carried patrons high above the ocean, providing a magnificent view of both the replica Arabian city below and the real host city above the palisades to the east. As a complement to the themed park, the Santa Monica Yacht and Motorboat Club offered moonlight rides alongside the pier.

Unfortunately, Dr. Wagner passed away just days before the opening of "The City of Baghdad." His widow, Lulu D. Wagner, assumed controlling interest of the pleasure pier. With no amusement experience to speak of, she immediately searched for someone to manage the Santa Monica Pier Amusement Company. In July 1928, she found Ernest Pickering.

Pickering was a familiar face in the area's amusement pier business, having been involved in amusement parks in Venice, Ocean Park, and San Bernardino. When Mrs. Wagner enticed him to Santa Monica, he marveled at the city's growth. He was instantly eager to assume management of the pier, which he referred to as the La Monica Pier to honor the pier's most notable attraction.

The pier's Baghdad theme was short-lived, and the pier eventually returned to a more traditional setting. Within a year, Pickering shifted the amusement pier's focus toward children. With sponsorship from the *Santa Monica Evening Outlook*, he organized beach parties on summer Saturdays, including free access to all of the amusements on the La Monica Pier. Featured entertainment included a "Punch and Judy" show, nighttime movies, and a high diver who made a ninety-seven-foot leap—complete with a back flip—into a tank of water.

In the winter of 1930, the effects of the nationwide Great Depression hit the pier. Unable to support the cost of their own maintenance, the Whirlwind Dipper and other amusement park rides were removed. Pickering, refusing to be discouraged by the nation's economic hardship, turned his focus to methods that would keep his amusements popular—and in place. In September 1931, the La Monica Pier hosted a fashion show and benefit to aid people on welfare.

In April 1931, Lulu Wagner and Pickering negotiated a twenty-one-year extension of the La Monica Pier's franchise. Two months later, they leased the pier to the Los Angeles Concession and Novelty Company, which focused on catering to the anticipated yacht harbor. Throughout the rest of the 1930s, the amusement pier was but a shell of itself, with little to qualify as "amusements." Wagner and Pickering repeatedly and unsuccessfully tried to sell the property to the city. Ultimately, they defaulted on their franchise lease, and Security First National Bank took over the property. The city considered purchasing the pier from Security First, but the ownership of the pier was tied up in legal red tape until the 1940s.

In 1924, new ownership of the pleasure pier installed the more exciting Whirlwind Dipper roller coaster, and extended the pier westward in order to support the new La Monica Ballroom.

The addition of rides and activities to Santa Monica's Municipal Pier in the early twentieth century firmly established Santa Monica as an iconic amusement center.

3 FROM THE DEPRESSION, NEW CULTURE IS BORN

*W*hile business enterprises worldwide, and certainly those on the pier, suffered from the impacts of the nation's economic crisis, the popularity of the pier and its adjacent beach thrived. And why not? Access was free, and the possibilities of prospective use were limited only by the imagination. Ingenuity flourished, especially on the beach where increasing multitudes of people gathered to enjoy Mother Nature's offerings for free. Volleyball found its way from the gymnasium to the beach, and, in 1930, the first-ever doubles beach volleyball game was played on the courts immediately south of the pier. A few years later, fitness and acrobatics enthusiasts created their own beach playground—also just south of the pier—and named it Muscle Beach. In the space between Muscle Beach and the pier, a new version of beach volleyball was created that changed the sport forever.

A young woman poses with an anchor-shaped flower arrangement for the official opening of Santa Monica Yacht Harbor on August 4, 1934. Opposite: A group of young women playfully inspect the new rock-mound breakwater during a media promotion shortly before the breakwater's completion.

Beach Volleyball

Volleyball was invented in 1895 in Holyoke, Massachusetts, and, in the 1920s, the sport found its way to the beach. Many beaches, in fact; Santa Monica is among the many beach communities that have claimed to be the location of the very first game of beach volleyball.

While the origins of beach volleyball remain in dispute, the history of doubles volleyball, in which each team has only two players instead of the usual six, is clear. The indisputable location of the very first doubles volleyball game was on the courts immediately south of Santa Monica Pier where, on a summer day in 1930, Paul "Pablo" Johnson, an established and respected player, was faced with the dilemma of striking up a game with only four competitors available. The result was a new, highly competitive version of volleyball in which the traditional advantage of height was countered by the more refined skills of speed and agility. Doubles beach volleyball quickly grew to become the most popular version due to its accessibility, relatively low number of participants, and excitement factor.

And the sport's birthplace—the beach courts just south of the pier—continued to thrive and attract some of the most talented and notable competitors in the sport's history, including Bobby Barber, Butch May and his daughter Misti, and Sinjin Smith. Another notable player regularly seen at the Santa Monica Pier courts, albeit famous for a completely different sport, was NBA legend Wilt Chamberlain.

Doubles beach volleyball has become one of the most popular beach sports in the world. Since it was added into the Summer Olympic Games in 1996, it has become arguably the most anticipated and most popular Olympic sport, often featuring athletes who have played on the original courts next to the pier.

As a result of their history, the pier courts are the host location of an annual tournament and celebration of the sport of doubles beach volleyball, which includes the formal induction of the sport's best individuals into the Beach Volleyball Legends Hall of Fame, presented by the California Beach Volleyball Association (CVBA).

On the north side of the pier, a construction project began to change everything on and around the pier. Dreams of a yacht harbor had always danced in Santa Monicans' heads. Plans were drawn up several times only to flounder before any real progress was actually made. Finally, in 1926, a group of businessmen formed the Santa Monica Breakwater Association and gained enough momentum to ask for state approval of breakwater and harbor construction.

In April 1929, the Breakwater Association lobbied the California State Senate to pass the Harbor District Bill—legislation that would allocate funding for the proposed breakwater. The bill required the signature of Governor Clement C. Young, and confidence was high that the project would move forward quickly. Enter the associates of newspaper magnate William Randolph Hearst, who were developing their own plans for a commercial harbor further up the coast and feared that a Santa Monica Yacht Harbor could potentially evolve into a commercial port. Despite strong assurances from the Breakwater Association that the harbor would not seek commercial interests, Governor Young vetoed the bill.

Undaunted, breakwater proponents persevered. An existing harbor bill still allowed for the construction of a small boat harbor with the support of public bonds. In June 1930, the Santa Monica City Council unanimously voted to build a breakwater and small boat harbor. Engineer Taggart Aston designed a breakwater that employed a series of sand-filled concrete caissons, each one hundred feet long, placed adjacent to one another to form a two-thousand-foot breakwater towering fourteen feet above the water line. The plans also called for an extension of the Municipal Pier and a bridge connecting the pier to the breakwater, allowing pedestrian access to it.

In September 1930, the Santa Monica Harbor Company, Ltd. was incorporated with an authorized capitalization of $2.5 million. Work began on October 28, 1930, with the extension of the Municipal Pier. The city held a ceremony for the commencement of the much-anticipated project, and ninety-four-year-old Mrs. D.G. Stephens, one of the bay area's first residents who was known locally as the "Mother of Santa Monica," directed the driving of the first pile. Mayor Herman Michel christened the pile with a soft drink bottle, and later that night, fireworks illuminated the sky.

By mid-February 1931, though, progress on the project came to a halt. The Santa Monica Harbor Company reported that its expected funding had fallen through. Their potential default left officials debating whether or not the city should build the breakwater. Earlier that month, the Santa Monica–Ocean Park Chamber of Commerce had reapplied to the state for an enabling act through which the breakwater could be financed. As if answering the city's prayers, the act passed the legislature and was signed by newly elected Governor James Rolph, Jr. on June 18, 1931, allowing Santa Monica to issue a district bond. A $690,000 bond measure was passed by popular vote on September 12, 1931, enabling the city to move forward with construction of the yacht harbor and the franchise contract with Santa Monica Harbor Company was canceled. The city chose to move forward with Taggart Aston's design for the breakwater.

The dock and forms were completed in February 1933, and the concrete for the first caisson was poured on

Top and Opposite: Beach volleyball games have been an everyday activity on the beach immediately south of Santa Monica Pier since the 1920s.

Santa Monica Pier and Yacht Harbor, 1935. Navy aircraft carrier USS *Saratoga* is anchored beyond the breakwater.

Muscle Beach

Not long after that seminal beach volleyball moment in 1930, another group of fitness and athletics-minded people sought to make the free and easily accessible beach their home. In 1932, Los Angeles hosted the Summer Olympic Games, and the very existence of the Games' athletic activity inspired many people to apply more focus to their own fitness. The open, spacious, and invigorating atmosphere of the beach drew such people, and since Santa Monica Beach was among the easiest Los Angeles area beaches to get to, the beach area south of the pier became a regular gathering place for like-minded fitness enthusiasts. Among those enthusiasts were a handful of circus-trained performers who would show off their talents with breathtaking feats, eventually drawing spectators to the area, which soon adopted the name Muscle Beach.

In 1934, a local physical education instructor named Kate Giroux convinced the City of Santa Monica to install a platform to better support the athletes and their feats. In short time, the tumbling and acrobatic performances at Muscle Beach became one of the area's most popular attractions, drawing thousands of people at a time to watch the development of human pyramids, multiperson handstand towers, balancing acts, and the catapulting of persons up into the air. The spectacle was truly amazing.

Fitness enthusiasts/gurus such as Joe Gold and Jack LaLanne were among those who regularly visited and ultimately thrived from their participation at Muscle Beach, with both becoming legends in the bodybuilding and fitness worlds. Likewise, Hollywood was drawn to displays of fitness and health, including highly notables like Roy Rogers and Kirk Douglas. With Hollywood, of course, comes broadened exposure, and the exposure that ensued from the activities at Muscle Beach cemented its reputation as the official "Birthplace of the Fitness Movement."

In 1958, following an unfortunate scandal, Santa Monica's Muscle Beach closed and the famous platformed area was dismantled and removed. A few years later, a new Muscle Beach opened in Venice, a few miles south of the original Santa Monica location, but with a focus more upon weightlifting and bodybuilding rather than the acrobatic performances of the Santa Monica days.

Still, the spirit of Santa Monica's Muscle Beach has managed to live on. Worldwide superstar bodybuilder/actor/politician Arnold Schwarzenegger, a longtime presence in Santa Monica, specifically chose to live and work out near the Santa Monica Pier when he immigrated to the United States from Austria in 1968, citing his reason for doing so was to associate himself with the official birthplace of fitness, Muscle Beach. To this day, he maintains an office within short walking distance of the iconic site.

Original Muscle Beach has seen a resurgence of its early spirit in recent years. While the tumbling platforms have yet to reappear, a new brand of athletic feats is featured daily. Aerial silks and slacklines now decorate the area, with skilled athletes performing feats comparable to those practiced in the heyday of the area's glorified past. Fitness instructors train classes for both groups and individuals daily, and the multitudes of passersby are still the great beneficiaries who get to witness and tell the story of how the fitness movement endures today, almost a century after Muscle Beach was born.

Gymnasts perform at Muscle Beach, just south of the Santa Monica Pier, 1942.

February 25. After setting and hardening for one month, it was towed to Santa Monica on March 25, two days earlier than expected. A surprised few witnessed the towing and spread the word so quickly that, by the time the caisson was placed, a large crowd had gathered on the end of the Municipal Pier to watch what was regarded as a pivotal moment in Santa Monica's history.

Less than a week later, a crack was discovered on the outer side of the newly placed caisson. Engineers originally thought collision with debris on the ocean floor when the caisson was dropped caused the crack, but further inspection revealed that a strong sea current was the real problem. To make matters worse, the ocean currents had carved out a forty-foot trough on both sides of the caissons base, causing the structure to settle an extra three feet. Construction of the remaining caissons was put on hold pending further investigation.

The city brought in United States Army Engineer D.E. Hughes to assess the situation. Hughes outlined shortcomings that he saw with the crib-type breakwater and advised building a rock-mound style instead. Taggart Aston defended his crib-type wall, arguing that a rock mound would cost in excess of $2 million. After researching the project thoroughly, officials determined that a rock-mound seawall was indeed within the amount budgeted, and on May 26, 1933, the city council formally approved the changes in the contract with the Puget Sound Bridge and Dredging Company.

Two barges brought the first thousand tons of stone from Santa Catalina Island on July 14, 1933, and deposited their loads into place, followed by a regular schedule of three barges arriving every other day, each carrying five hundred tons of stone. In late September, a derrick barge arrived for placement of the heavier rock, called "armor stone," atop the base of the rock wall. By early October, the rock wall was finally visible to people looking from the beach and the pier.

On a rainy December 14, 1933, John "Scotty" McPherson accidentally fell into the tow of a 150-ton load of rock as it was poured into place on the rock mound.

Only twenty-seven years old, McPherson was a well-liked local fisherman who had taken temporary work on the breakwater to make ends meet. Two days after the accident, a deep-sea diver found his body snagged on the top of the breakwater mound twenty feet below the surface. At the request of the rest of the work crew, arrangements were made to place a bronze memorial tablet on one of the breakwater stones to honor him. Safety measures were tightened and, though there were a couple of other minor accidents as the project progressed, McPherson was the breakwater's only casualty.

On July 30, the city council announced the completion of the breakwater, adopted an ordinance for boating regulations, and appointed lifeguard captains George Watkins, Owen Churchill, and George Mills to the Harbor Committee. The breakwater completion came just in time. Santa Monica officials had long before agreed to host the first annual Santa Monica Regatta on August 4. The construction barges were quickly cleared for the regatta while the city held a special dedication ceremony for the new harbor.

In the mid-1910s, public enjoyment of ocean waters began to increase significantly as beachgoers became increasingly emboldened to leave the safety of the paci-

fied waters provided by bathhouses—where ocean water was pumped into beachside pools for people to enjoy—to instead try their swimming skills in the invigorating saltwater in its natural environment and accompanying surf. Hawaiian-born George Freeth, who today is widely recognized as the person who, in 1907, first introduced surfing to the mainland United States, was also a highly skilled lifeguard whose experience and innovation helped to greatly advance ocean lifesaving techniques. In 1916, two other skilled ocean enthusiasts, Thomas Sheffield and George "Cap" Watkins, with support from the Red Cross, established a volunteer lifeguard force in Santa Monica to protect the beach-going public from the natural forces of the ocean. Watkins became well known and instantly recognizable for patrolling the beach while riding a horse, a concept that would later modernize with motor vehicles and become symbolic in the influential nature of Santa Monica's lifeguard service.

In the mid-1920s, the steady increase of the previous decade became a surge, and along with it came the need for more and better structured lifesaving measures, especially during the warm summer months. With the economic collapse of the Great Depression in the late 1920s, the surge became an explosion. Santa Monica city officials recognized the need for a paid, full-time lifeguard force and, in April 1932, created the Santa Monica Lifeguard Service, naming George Watkins as captain and determining locations for a number of lifeguard stations—each built by recently unemployed Santa Monicans—along the beach. Needing a headquarters for this new department, the city secured space in the Bowling & Billiards Building, which had recently become vacant. In 1935, that headquarters was moved to the west end of the pier as the lifeguard force grew in both staff size and overall stature.

Throughout its history, the Santa Monica Lifeguard Service boasted some of the most talented, respected, and innovative watermen that the world has ever known. Among their ranks were Preston "Pete" Peterson, Tommy Zahn, Wally Burton, and Paul Stader, each of whom established reputations not only as highly skilled watermen, but also as gifted surfboard shapers and watercraft builders. They even drew the attention and appreciation of Hollywood, which relied greatly upon their expertise as both stuntmen and expert advisors. The attraction was reciprocal, for actors/Olympians Buster Crabbe and Johnny Weissmuller so frequently visited with the Santa Monica crew that they were ultimately initiated as honorary lifeguards. Weissmuller even nabbed headlines in a couple of ocean rescues—in 1933, he leapt off the pier to save a swimmer from drowning, and, in 1943, made a beach rescue about one hundred yards north of the pier.

Left: Santa Monica lifeguards, including paddleboard innovator Tom Blake (wearing a hat) and Preston "Pete" Peterson (bottom), paddle on Blake-designed hollow boards, 1932. Right: The same Santa Monica Lifeguards exercise their surfing skills.

A Waterman Without Equal
Preston "Pete" Peterson

Mention the name Pete Peterson to any lifeguard or surf history buff and you'll likely hear them comment that he was the "greatest waterman who ever lived." His skills and reputation certainly make him worthy of the title.

One of the original crew members of the Santa Monica Lifeguard Service, Peterson served briefly during the summer of 1928, before it was discovered that he was underage—he was only fifteen at the time. Upon turning sixteen, the legal working age, he rejoined and, but for a stint serving in the United States Navy during the Second World War, enjoyed a career as a lifeguard until 1955.

Peterson's skills translated to much more than water rescue, though. He was exceptionally skilled at swimming, surfing, paddleboarding, rowing, sailing, SCUBA diving, boating, water skiing—anything to do with the ocean! In 1932, he competed against friendly rivals Tom Blake and Wally Burton in the first-ever paddleboard race from the mainland (Point Vicente) to Catalina, then traveled to the Hawaiian island of Oahu and became one of the first "haoles" ever to surf the island's now-famous north shore, and then wrapped up that fantastic year by earning the crown as first-ever Pacific Coast Surfing Champion—a feat that he accomplished again in 1936, 1938, and 1941. He also competed regularly and earned championship titles in paddleboard, swim, and dory racing.

During the Second World War, he was recruited into the United States Navy as a fitter and diver, serving on the USS *Pandemus* in the Philippines, Saipan, Iwo Jima, and Okinawa. When he returned from the war, he resumed his career as a lifeguard and artisan. He built high-quality lifeguard dories and skiffs, and was one of the first—if not the first—to develop the hollow fiberglass surfboard, an innovation that paved the way for modern-day surfboard technology. He also helped create and manufacture the widely utilized lifesaving Peterson Rescue Tube.

Hollywood regularly called upon Peterson throughout his career to perform stunt work and small acting roles for feature films and television. Among his movie and television credits are *Voyage to the Bottom of the Sea* (1961), *Poseidon Adventure* (1972), and *Jaws* (1975).

After his retirement from the lifeguard force, Peterson opened a workshop at the west end of the Santa Monica Pier. Here he exercised his skills as a craftsman, creating wooden surfboards and paddleboards that are highly coveted by contemporary collectors. He also performed expert repair and maintenance on local boats and yachts. Sadly, his shop and much of his handiwork was destroyed along with the entire west end of the pier in the catastrophic winter storms of 1983. He passed away just a couple of months later.

For a short time in 1932, surf pioneer Tom Blake joined the Santa Monica Lifeguard Service, and while his time with them was brief, it was not without great significance. A Wisconsin native, Blake moved to Hawaii in 1924 to pursue the island lifestyle he learned about several years earlier through a traveling water sports exhibition featuring Olympic gold medalist Duke Kahanamoku.

When Blake arrived in Waikiki, he encountered the native sport of surfing, which was at that time experiencing a resurgence in popularity. Naturally, Blake became an enthusiast. At that time, surfboards were made of solid wood and were extraordinarily heavy—well over one hundred pounds—and difficult to maneuver. Blake made it his personal mission to solve these issues. As a result, he invented the hollow board, which he patented in 1930. By 1932, his patented board design had been picked up by a number of manufacturing companies; among them was the Rogers Company of Venice, California. Blake returned to the mainland to supervise the work of the Rogers Company and, during his time in the Los Angeles area, joined the Santa Monica Lifeguard Service. While there, he introduced his new hollow boards, crafted by the Rogers Company, to his fellow lifeguards, who adopted the hollow paddleboard as one of their primary lifesaving tools. Paddleboards were soon a standard part of every lifeguard service along the California coast.

The innovation did not stop with paddleboards. When the lifeguard service was founded in 1932, the City of Santa Monica installed telephone lines connecting each lifeguard tower for direct communications, the first such use for a lifeguard service. In 1940, the lifeguards began using radios between their headquarters on the end of the Santa Monica Pier and their boat, the *Palama Kai*. In 1910, long before the establishment of the Santa Monica Life-

guard Service, "Cap" Watkins set a trend by patrolling the beach as a volunteer in the fastest and most efficient way he knew how—using his horse. By the 1940s, this approach was upgraded to a more modern approach when Watkins and his Santa Monica crew acquired two off-road four-wheel drive jeeps for the same purpose. And yet, all of those incredibly important innovations pale in comparison to the one invention that has probably saved more lives than all of those thus far mentioned.

In 1935, Santa Monica lifeguard "Pete" Peterson crafted an inflatable rescue tube, originally conceived by fellow Santa Monica lifeguards Reggie Burton and "Cap"

Top: The Santa Monica lifeguards, assembled in front of their original 1932 headquarters. Bottom: The lifeguards in front of their second headquarters location at the La Monica Ballroom.

Watkins. Up to this point, the techniques for ocean rescues were almost solely body-to-body, with an expert swimmer using their body to support both themselves and the victim. Landlines—running a cable from shore to victim—were used to modest effect, and the donut-shaped life ring popularized in East Coast states proved successful when applied from boats, yet far less effective in beach rescue operations due to the distance that a lifesaver often had to throw the ring. A steel, torpedo-shaped lifesaving "rescue can" was developed in the late nineteenth century by Thomas Sheffield (one of the Santa Monica lifeguard originators), and was early standard fare for lifeguard services. But it was this new inflatable rubber tube that became the "game-changer," for its flexible, bendable qualities enabled a rescuer to wrap the buoyant tube around the

troubled swimmer, and then connect the tube via clasps at each end, creating a flotation device that could always keep a victim's head above water. A rope attached at one end of the tube allowed the rescuer to effectively tow the victim to shore. The tube became known as the Peterson Rescue Tube. In 1964, utilizing the same design as the inflatable tube, Peterson solved the only persistent problem with the inflatable version—deflation—by creating a foam tube, covered with a thin layer of rubber. This new, red-orange rescue tube instantly became the industry standard for lifesaving tools, and can still be seen today at swimming pools, lakesides, and ocean beaches worldwide.

Renowned for rescue and safety abilities, the lifeguards contributed to the community in many other capacities. They staged demonstrations and held competi-

tions to keep themselves fit and well trained, as well as to entertain beach and pier-goers. When the much-anticipated yacht harbor opened in 1934, Captain Watkins and his guards were called upon to establish rules and regulations to keep the harbor safe. Guards dove for abalone and lobsters, donating their catch to the community to ease the food shortages Santa Monica residents faced during the Second World War.

During the war, many Santa Monica guards were recruited for service, most often by the United States Navy.

The note accompanying this photo in Santa Monica Mayor Edmond Gillette's scrapbook read "Twenty-one reasons why Santa Monica is considered the safest beach in California."

In 1942, President Franklin Delano Roosevelt created the Office of Strategic Services (OSS) for special intelligence operations. The new organization enlisted the services of Los Angeles-area dentist Jack Taylor, who in turn gathered a team of skilled watermen, including some Santa Monica lifeguards, for special and secret service. The OSS ceased operation after the conclusion of the Second World War, but is widely recognized as the precursor of both the Central Intelligence Agency (CIA) and United States Navy Seals.

Post-war lifeguard service saw a return to thriving beach activity and, with it, a surge in popularity of Southern California beach culture brought on largely by Hollywood movies and television shows. The guards maintained their chief presence on the pier until 1958, when a

Tarzan was at the Pier

On August 11, 1933, ten-year-old Bobby Wheeler was swimming next to the Santa Monica Pier when his foot got tangled in a string of loose kelp. In his mind, he was doomed. He screamed for help at the top of his lungs as he thrashed in the water. From atop the pier, a hero dove thirty feet down into the sea, then surfaced next to him. Bobby couldn't believe his eyes when he looked into his hero's familiar face. It couldn't be, could it? Indeed it was…His hero was Tarzan.

Johnny Weissmuller made his mark in the world in two fantastic arenas—competitive swimming and the silver screen. Winner of five Olympic gold medals in the 1924 and 1928 games, fifty-two US national champions and sixty-seven world records, his feats in the water have stood unparalleled for nearly a century. His post-swimming career landed him in Hollywood, where he immortalized the legendary Edgar Rice Boroughs's character "Tarzan" in twelve films, including the 1932 classic *Tarzan of the Apes*. He is easily one of the most recognizable watermen ever to have lived, and he was very often recognized at the Santa Monica Pier!

Johnny loved Santa Monica and its magnificent pier. He trained often with the Santa Monica lifeguards in the 1930s in order to keep himself in top physical condition for his movie appearances. His water skills were put to the test several times with a few impromptu—and always successful—rescues. His talent and willingness to risk his life to rescue others prompted lifeguard chief "Cap" Watkins to induct him as an Honorary Santa Monica lifeguard.

In the 1940s, Johnny happened upon the pier's meteorically popular new Manoa Paddleboard Club. This fun-loving, talented group of youngsters gladly welcomed him into the club and Johnny found new workout partners to challenge him and keep him physically fit. He invited his Hollywood friends, stuntman Stubby Kreuger and fellow actor Johnny Sheffield ("Boy" in the Tarzan films), to join as well, making the Manoa club even more of a public draw.

Visitors to the pier during those days could enjoy not only watching incredible paddleboarding feats, but also hearing the occasional Tarzan yell ("aah- aaahaahaa-aa-haah!") and see a man swing from the clubhouse rope out over the beautiful Santa Monica Bay. It couldn't be, could it? Indeed it was… Johnny Weissmuller.

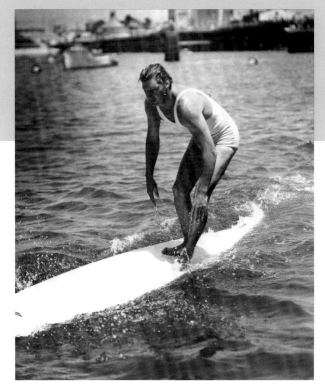

new headquarters was built just south of the pier. In 1974, the City of Santa Monica relinquished its control of the lifeguards and turned the service over to the supervision of Los Angeles County. The Los Angeles County Lifeguard Service continues utilizing the innovations developed by the Santa Monica service, as do lifesaving organizations throughout the world.

Olympic athlete and Tarzan actor Johnny Weissmuller shows off his surfing skills next to the pier. Opposite: Young women enjoy a moment atop the new breakwater at Santa Monica Yacht Harbor.

4

WAR ABROAD, LEAN YEARS ON THE PIER

anta Monica Yacht Harbor was extraordinarily popular in its early years. No sooner was it complete than motion picture star Charlie Chaplin moored his yacht *Panacea* (although rather than use his own name, he registered it under the name of his soon-to-be bride Paulette Goddard). By the end of August 1934, the harbor already boasted ninety-nine yacht moorings. Sailboats were a regular sight in the protective calm provided by the new breakwater, and many beach bathers found the water less of a challenge on the north side of the Municipal Pier since the breakwater controlled the waves. New restaurants such as O.J. Bennett's Seafood Grotto and The Galley thrived as a result of its presence. Likewise, shops for boat rentals, repair, parts, and maintenance cropped up on the pier deck. The newly formed Santa Monica Lifeguard Service established their headquarters on the pier, and their use of the immensely innovative hollow

A postcard of popular restaurant O.J. Bennett's Sea Food Grotto, 1930s. Opposite: Aerial image of Santa Monica Pier and beach, circa 1932.

Santa Monica Yacht Harbor opened on August 4, 1934, and was immediately popular among the boating community.

paddleboard, designed by waterman Tom Blake, as a life-saving and training tool inspired civilians to try their skills on paddleboards. It didn't take long for paddleboard races to become a new source of fun for participants and spectators alike.

The environment changed as well. The presence of the breakwater affected the ocean's natural current and the beach accumulated sand at an alarming rate, expanding the beach to more than three times its normal width. This, of course, was problematic in that the intent of the harbor was as a revenue stream for the City of Santa Monica, yet the need to dredge the accumulating sand out of the new harbor in order to maintain its area for mooring space became an unexpected and frustrating expense.

In the summer of 1935, the steamship *Cabrillo* offered daily service to Santa Catalina Island, much to the dismay of many yachtsmen who felt that the large ship's path through the harbor would take up too much valuable mooring space. As if answering the yachting community's prayers, heavy swells often prevented the *Cabrillo* from accessing the harbor. Ultimately, interest in the Catalina service faded, and operations shut down altogether the following August, though they resumed briefly aboard the ship *Narconian III* in the late 1930s.

In the mid-1930s, people could embark upon cruises to Santa Catalina Island from the pier. Opposite: The yacht harbor and its water-pacifying breakwater had a tremendous impact on beach life, luring crowds of people and their ocean vessels.

The Battle of Santa Monica Bay

In Raymond Chandler's 1940 novel *Farewell, My Lovely,* the fictional town of Bay City, based on Santa Monica of the 1930s, is immersed in corruption and gambling, complete with casino barges anchored just off the end of the pier. It wasn't far from the truth. There's been a history of gambling linked to the seaside area, and the pier was no innocent bystander. Tales are still told about games of chance hosted in the secret backrooms of some of the pier's former establishments. One such story tells of a man winning heavily at craps until someone discovered his dice were loaded. The fool was dragged outside and thrown off the pier into the ocean. But Chandler truly captures the era when he writes about the bay's gambling ships, a memorable part of the pier's history.

The first of the Santa Monica Bay gambling barges, the *Johanna Smith*, appeared in the summer of 1929. Anchored thirteen miles off the Santa Monica shore, the commute to reach her via taxi boats from the Venice Pier took nearly two hours. Poor attendance forced the barge out of business. Other barges appeared, then disappeared for various reasons until mobster Tony Cornero arrived with a small fleet of "floating casinos." The most infamous was the *SS Rex.*

Rex was no stranger to the area. For many years, Captain Charles Arnold operated her as a fishing barge named *Star of Scotland.* In 1938, when Cornero bought her, the mobster converted the ship into a deluxe floating resort, and anchored the *Rex* 3.1 miles offshore, just off the end of the Santa Monica Pier, and outside the three-mile legal boundary for gambling operations. A collection of fast shore boats could get passengers from the pier to the *Rex* in about ten minutes. When operations began on May 5, 1938, the *Rex* brought more people to the pier than anyone dreamed.

The city did not share the pleasure of Cornero and his patrons, however. After the *Rex* opened—and even before—the city fought for months, several times closing off the water taxi operations offered at the pier. After every closure, Cornero managed to find new loopholes that allowed service to the *Rex* to return to the pier. City commissioners ultimately appealed to District Attorney Earl Warren to intervene.

On July 28,1939, Warren declared that the legal jurisdiction line for gambling begins not at a distance of three miles from shore, but three miles from an imaginary line drawn from Point Vicente to Point Dume. Operators of the gambling ships remained defiant, so Warren ordered officers to raid the ships and arrest the personnel aboard them. The *Rex* was the last to surrender, holding officers at bay for eight days by spraying water at intruding law enforcement boats using the ship's high-powered fire hoses. The standoff at the time was referred to as "The Battle of Santa Monica Bay." Finally, on August 10, 1939, Cornero surrendered, telling the press, "I needed a haircut." Months later, officials boarded the ship and destroyed all of its gaming equipment. In the process, they discovered that most of the machines had been rigged. The patrons of the *SS Rex* never had a sporting chance.

The king of all of the infamous gambling ships, SS *Rex*, the flagship of mobster Tony Cornero.

The Origins of Paddleboard Racing

When the Santa Monica Lifeguards adopted the Tom Blake-designed, Rogers Company paddleboards as part of their arsenal of lifesaving equipment, it didn't take long for the public to notice and admire the new boards. The lifeguards regularly trained in the pier-adjacent water, and it's difficult to miss seeing an attractive, finely crafted fourteen-foot-long paddleboard gliding through the ocean with one of Santa Monica's finest first responders aboard it. By the time the breakwater for Santa Monica's new yacht harbor was complete and effectively pacifying the local water in the summer of 1934, every skilled ocean enthusiast wanted to ride a paddleboard.

The Santa Monica Athletic Club was among the first to organize races within the newly finished harbor, ultimately reaching out to challenge other private beach clubs along the coast to match paddleboard racing talents, with Santa Monica Yacht Harbor becoming known as an ideal location for paddleboard racing.

The general beach-going public was equally interested, and paddleboard rental businesses popped up all along the California coastline. One such rental operation was located directly underneath Santa Monica Pier's O.J. Bennett's Seafood Grotto, immediately adjacent and accessible to the new yacht harbor. A public paddleboard club called Hui Maiokioki was created, with its clubhouse on the pier.

Highly anticipated annual events featuring paddleboard racing highlighted the Santa Monica Bay events calendar throughout the 1940s, including the Pacific Coast Surfing and Paddleboard Championship and an annual race from the mainland to Catalina, inspired by a friendly 1932 competition between Santa Monica lifeguards Tom Blake, Pete Peterson, and Wally Burton. Among the most notable paddleboard racers of the 1940s and 1950s was another Santa Monica lifeguard, Tommy Zahn, whose talents alone kept the sport of paddleboard racing alive for many years.

Ultimately, though, paddleboard racing's popularity succumbed to the much more exciting water sport of competitive surfing, and in the 1950s, the sport that inspired so many people to get into the water in the late 1930s and 1940s largely disappeared.

In the early 2000s, a new approach to the sport—stand-up paddleboard (also known as SUP)—quickly became popular, and races once again became a favorite competitive event. In 2010, the Santa Monica Pier joined the excitement and held a paddleboard race, which has since grown into the pier's annual kickoff to summer event, the pier 360 Beach Festival.

Paddleboard culture developed in the breakwater-pacified waters next to the pier in the mid-1930s.

Dottie Hawkins
And the Hui Maiokioki Paddleboard Club

Ed Hawkins had a keen sense for talent. Or perhaps he was just trying to be the best father he knew how to be. His job as a film runner for movie studios allowed him the time after his work shift to pick up his daughter Dorothy, nicknamed Dottie, from school every day and take her to Santa Monica Beach where he would exercise at Muscle Beach on the south side of the pier and, afterward, rent paddleboards for both to enjoy on the north side of the pier. In the summer of 1939, recognizing that nine-year-old Dottie was pretty well skilled on her paddleboard, Ed entered her into an all-ages ocean paddleboard race at Ballona Creek, a few miles south of the pier. The only child competing against a field that totally consisted of adult women, Dottie finished in third place!

Inspired by the talents of his daughter, Ed sought to foster her talent and keep her involved in competitive paddleboard racing. However, most races at the time were organized by private beach clubs, which the Hawkins family could ill afford to join. Ed turned to "Cap" Watkins of the Santa Monica Lifeguards, whom he had known casually, for advice. Coincidentally, the Lifeguards had an underutilized storage space on the lower level of the pier's west end, which "Cap" Watkins felt could be a good clubhouse for a new, affordable paddleboard club. A deal was agreed upon, and Ed Hawkins founded the public paddleboard club Hui Maiokioki. This new club offered twenty-five-cent-a-day paddleboard rentals and affordable lessons and challenged local private clubs to race. Dottie, the young prodigy, competed regularly and never finished a race at less than first place.

Ed recognized the value of spectacle and, working in partnership with members of the Santa Monica Paddleboard Club whom he had become friendly with, created a special Hui Maiokioki initiation ceremony to be performed specifically for an audience at the pier in late January 1941. Media outlets were invited, and among those that showed were the *Santa Monica Evening Outlook* and *PIC Magazine*, the latter publication featuring the day's events in a four-page spread in its July 1941 issue. The event included a ceremonial parade of paddleboards and outrigger canoes winding their way through the yacht harbor and ultimately arriving at a decorated barge near the pier. Members newly joining the club were then blindfolded and thrown into the ocean from the barge, after which all members participated in races throughout the rest of the day.

Top: Young Dottie Hawkins shows off her prowess on a paddleboard. Center: Membership card for the Manoa Surf Club (originally named Hui Maiokioki) and racing medals from the Southern Pacific Association Paddleboard Championships in the early 1940s. Bottom: Manoa Surf Club paddleboarders (from left to right) Eleanor Moynier, Dottie Hawkins, and Janet Dee, 1946.

A couple of years later, the club changed their name to the less tongue-twisting, but still very Hawaiian-influenced, Manoa Surf Club. Their regular activities in Santa Monica Yacht Harbor became a regular draw for pier visitors as well as for Hollywood celebrities, with notables such as Burgess Meredith and Johnny Weissmuller joining the fun. Dottie, being the best racer and easily the most skilled paddleboarder, became sought after as a trainer, and Weissmuller was among her students. During his time with the Manoa club, Weissmuller made a handful of films including *Tarzan Triumphs*, *Tarzan's Desert Mystery*, *Tarzan and the Amazons*, and *Tarzan and the Leopard Woman*. As each of these film productions approached, Weissmuller needed to get into top physical condition, and paddleboarding was a great way to do so. Needing a trainer to help him get into shape, he regularly called upon young Dottie, who would challenge him and make him work harder than he could do by himself.

The Manoa club heightened its reputation even further by creating events such as paddleboard water polo and paddleboard water ballet, for which Dottie had the dual role of choreographer and lead performer. As the Second World War drew to a close in the mid-1940s, the Manoa Paddleboard Ballet became a featured act both at the pier and at local swim clubs and festivals. Joining the country's patriotic enthusiasm at the time, the ballet boards, which had been designed and built by Ed Hawkins and his young protégé Tommy Volk, were painted in a red, white, and blue stars and stripes motif.

In 1947, seventeen-year-old Dottie left the Manoa club after an altercation with her father and simultaneously feeling compelled to move on. With the person who inspired him to create the club in the first place gone, Ed turned over the Manoa Surf Club operations to Janet Dee, whose daughter Jo Anne was a club member (and ultimately won the honor of being Miss Santa Monica). Janet Dee carried forth with the Manoa Paddleboard Ballet's popularity as a touring performance group and booked the group for a European tour with Buster Crabbe's International Ocean Festival and, after that, several years with Larry Crosby's Aquacade (Larry being entertainer Bing Crosby's younger brother).

Top Left: Manoa Paddleboard Water Ballet performance, featuring "Miss Santa Monica" Janet Dee. Top Right: Hui Maiokioki paddleboard club gathers for a membership initiation event next to the pier. Club founder Ed Hawkins in the foreground, wearing a captain's hat; 1941. Bottom: Manoa Paddleboard Water Ballet team members, 1946.

With the outbreak of the Second World War came the virtual end of the harbor's relationship with the yachting community. United States naval activities displaced entire fleets of fishing boats moored in Los Angeles, Newport, and San Diego harbors, forcing them to relocate to smaller harbors. By December 15, 1941, forty-six of these boats found a home in Santa Monica and embarked upon a very successful business. Tons of mackerel were hauled in daily, unloaded at the Municipal Pier onto cargo trucks, and shipped out to canneries in San Pedro. As luck would have it, business became too good. The pier deck and substructure took a substantial beating from the large trucks. In September 1942, city officials lowered the legal vehicle-weight limit from five tons to three tons, a crippling blow to the fishing industry. The inability to ship their haul from the pier forced many boats to dump their day's catch into the bay rather than let it rot in their boats. In early October 1942, as much as ten thousand tons of dead mackerel littered the harbor waters. The United States Department of War intervened and ordered emergency repairs to be made to accommodate the trucks and resume operations.

The yachting community, for whom the harbor was built, was overlooked in the fishing rush. Years of storms had damaged the breakwater enough that the harbor's waters were no longer optimal for mooring, and the city was slow to begin repairs. Yacht owners began to depart for more amenable anchorage.

Rebellion! Commercial fishing crews toss their fish hauls into the bay to protest Santa Monica's short-lived vehicle restrictions, which effectively closed the pier's seafood distribution operations.

At the end of the war, the status of the breakwater drew significant attention. Los Angeles officials made a formal plea to have the breakwater removed because of its negative erosion effects on southern beaches, a call that infuriated Santa Monica officials. Commissioners D.C. Freeman and W.W. Milliken pointed out that the removal of the breakwater would jeopardize the safety of the Santa Monica Pier. The commissioners posed the question that, if Santa Monica were to eventually lose both of these structures, "What has Santa Monica left in the way of beach identity?" No action was taken on the Los Angeles plea.

By the late 1940s, the majority of boats that braved the harbor's increasingly choppy waters were fishing boats. Efforts to regain the interest of the yachting community were unsuccessful. While a few yachts did remain, even they moved on over time. Ongoing dredging and repair costs became a financial drain on the city, and, by the early 1980s, little was left of the breakwater and Santa Monica Yacht Harbor.

Likewise, the businesses broadly struggled—even those which hoped to benefit from the new harbor.

By 1940, the amusement pier faced an identity crisis. It was no longer home to crowds of people laughing and screaming aboard its thrill rides. Instead, the pier found more use as a parking lot bordered by a small collection of businesses. By default, Security First National Bank held title to the franchise. The bankers continually tried to find

Left: Santa Monica Yacht Harbor's tugboat Malahat with Captain Chad Merrill aboard, 1952. Right: Aerial view of Santa Monica Pier and Yacht Harbor, 1934.

suitors interested in purchasing the franchise, but to no avail. They hired Harold Walker, a former officer in the U.S. Navy, to manage the pier, who in turn invited his close friend Walter D. Newcomb, Jr., to be co-manager. At the time, Newcomb owned the Venice Pier Fun House and merry-go-round. When World War II broke out in 1941, Commander Walker rejoined the Navy, leaving Newcomb to manage the pier on his own. Newcomb eventually purchased the franchise in March 1943.

Upon purchasing the Santa Monica Amusement Pier, Newcomb boasted that he had big plans for the venue, but since the nation was in the middle of wartime restrictions, those plans would have to wait. The ballroom, restaurants, and shops prospered during the war, the residual effect of the high-volume fishing operations on both piers. Newcomb sought to capitalize on the booming fishing industry by adding a new hoist at the end of his pier, to increase the high volume of production already being shipped through Santa Monica.

When the war ended, Newcomb found himself in an enviable position. The amusement business was expected to see a great surge with the return of the country's

The lower deck of the pier's west end became a beloved gathering place for ocean enthusiasts, including the paddleboarding community, seen here in the early 1940s.

Left: Enid Newcomb, circa 1960s. Right: Spade Cooley, "The King of Western Swing", was the pier's top-drawing musical performer in the late 1940s.

military personnel and a general feeling of national pride. Plus, the closure of the Venice Pier reduced his competition. He relocated his Venice-based carousel into the old Looff Hippodrome and focused on maintaining a steady home in his ballroom for an increasingly popular musician named Spade Cooley. He also added some new, smaller rides to accompany his existing penny arcade and gift shop.

In 1952, Newcomb entered negotiations for a new twenty-one year lease for the franchise, making it easier to secure funding to add new attractions to his pier. The city, acting with wary foresight, inserted the provision that upon expiration of the lease, Newcomb would be responsible for tearing the property down. Newcomb agreed, securing his ownership of the franchise until the early 1970s.

On June 11, 1954, while vacationing in Europe with his wife Enid, Walter Newcomb suddenly died, his hopes of expanding amusement operations unfulfilled. He left his estate, including operation of the pier, to Enid and their two daughters, Elizabeth and Jane.

When it came to the professional world, Enid Newcomb was no novice. In addition to being a wife and mother, she was a college graduate and small-business owner. Prior to Walter's death, she operated the gift shop on the pier, and when Walter passed away, she handled the transition into managing the pier and wrangling with Santa Monica politics rather easily. Still, she recognized that manage-

ment of the pier was a demanding task, so she sought help from longtime family friend Morris "Pops" Gordon. Gordon was an affluent Santa Monica businessman known for his success with penny arcades and other small enterprises. When he was approached by Mrs. Newcomb, he offered the services of his sons, George and Eugene. The hardworking Gordon sons took over the management responsibilities of the carousel and both penny arcades. Under Enid Newcomb's leadership, the pier continued its operations, first under the name of the Santa Monica Pier Company, and, later, under Bay Amusement Corporation.

Throughout the 1960s and 1970s, the Newcomb and Municipal Piers—by then commonly referred to jointly as Santa Monica Pier—were noticeably aging. Compared to neighboring Pacific Ocean Park (POP) pier a mile south and Disneyland in Anaheim, the vintage pier bordered on seedy. Nevertheless, while observers agree that these years were the pier's worst era, they were the years that its character took shape. Artists frequented the pier; some lived in apartments above the carousel and in the old ballroom. People could roam its decks without the assault of flash and action found in amusement parks, but with plenty of sound and energy. The pier had become a small neighborhood, hovering peacefully above the sand and sea.

Popeye

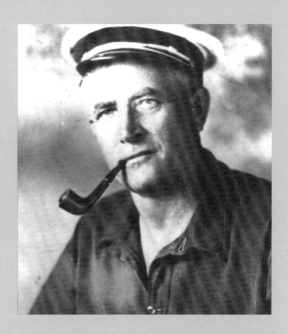

Popeye was a regular on the Santa Monica Pier. It's true! His creator, Elzie Crisler, aka E.C. Segar, visited the pier daily in the 1930s, renting a skiff where he and his assistant would discuss story ideas for his King Features comic strip *Thimble Theatre*. They rented their daily boat from Captain Olaf C. Olsen, a big-hearted retired sailor whose wardrobe and smoking pipe caught the eye of the popular cartoonist. While the true character inspiration for Popeye is often credited to Frank "Rocky" Fiegel, a memorable ruffian from Segar's youth in Illinois, one glimpse of a photo of Olsen clearly shows the physical inspiration.

A remarkable man in his own right, Olsen was born in 1879 in Norway, where he grew up aboard sailing ships. He immigrated to the United States as a teenager and joined the U.S. Navy. After finishing his service, he continued sailing until he settled in Santa Monica in 1925. He bought an old whaling ship called the *Narwhal* and converted her to a fishing barge, the first in a fleet of barges, day boats, and water taxis that he operated from the pier. He became an instrumental figure in the early development of Santa Monica Bay's pleasure fishing industry.

Olsen was passionate about the rights of sport fishermen and the health of the local ecosystem. In 1928, he led the first campaign to protect marine life in Santa Monica Bay. Commercial fishing boats, he feared, were on the verge of wiping out the population of local fish and upsetting the bay's ecological balance. His crusade initially resulted in a ban on net fishing, and, ultimately, in a ban on all commercial fishing in the bay.

In the early 1930s, the city granted Olsen a franchise to manage all boating operations on the Municipal Pier, a very important position given the popularity of sport fishing. A compassionate man, he invited men from the Unemployed Citizens League to fish from his boats and barges for free during the Great Depression. When he could, he donated a percentage of his own catch to those in need. His big heart overshadowed his business sense, however. In three-and-a-half years of management, Olsen never once paid rent, and the city revoked his franchise. Despite his ouster, he remained a vivid presence on the pier and in the local sport fishing scene. Like any fisherman worth his salt, he was never without a good story, and bent the ears of children and adults alike until he passed away in 1950.

Top: Captain Olaf C, Olsen, operator of a fleet of the pier's fishing boats, was the physical inspiration for Popeye."

During the pier's first seven decades, visitors could drive their cars all the way to the end of the pier.

Santa Monica Pier and Yacht Harbor, 1958.

5

SAVE THE PIER!

"Tear down the pier and you tear the heart out of Santa Monica!"
—Unidentified voice at Santa Monica City Council meeting; January 23, 1973

For nearly sixty-four years, nobody dreamed it could happen. The notion that the city would tear down Santa Monica Pier, a structure that it owned and that offered free pleasure to its citizens, had never really entered anyone's mind. Furthermore, it was the last of the famous pleasure piers that once lined the Southern California coast. If anything, it was a monument. Nobody would be crazy enough to tear down a monument. But there it was in the newspapers, there it was on the television, and there it was on the Santa Monica City Council dais: The pier, the heart of Santa Monica, was going to be torn down.

To the city council members, the idea seemed sound enough. The Municipal Pier and breakwater had been a financial drain for years, and each was in a state of such disrepair that the cost of salvage and restoration was becoming increasingly unrealistic. Furthermore, the

Community organizers proactively distributed pins to rally grassroots support to save the pier from demolition in 1973. Opposite: An image from an invitation to a fundraiser party to save the pier from demolition.

83

the Santa Monica Causeway

Newcomb Pier's lease was set to expire in 1973, and provisions in the lease called for demolition within six months of expiration.

Major changes to the harbor had been discussed as early as 1963, when hopes to convert the breakwater into a causeway connecting Santa Monica to Malibu surfaced and received considerable local support. Plans for the causeway ultimately fell through, and in 1971, the city council turned to City Manager Perry Scott to come up with a solution to improve the pier and harbor area. Scott returned to the council in November 1971 with a proposal for a thirty-five-acre island featuring a high-rise hotel, a convention center, restaurants, and several other amenities. What Scott's plan did not include was the pier. He

In the 1960s, officials dreamed of a causeway to replace the existing Pacific Coast Highway, creating a more direct route from Santa Monica to Malibu. Opposite: An impassioned crowd of citizens gathered at Santa Monica City Hall to protest the 1973 city council decision to tear down the Santa Monica Pier.

proposed that the pier be torn down in favor of a four-lane bridge that would provide access to and from the island. On June 13, 1972, the city council unanimously approved the project.

The public reacted immediately. Citizens of Santa Monica and West Los Angeles formed *Save the Santa Monica Bay*, a campaign endorsed by local environmental groups including the Sierra Club, and rallied enough support to ensure that the project would not receive the required state and national approvals necessary to proceed. By the following December, the city council began to suspect that the island, like the causeway a decade earlier, might be a futile pursuit. At their January 9, 1973 meeting, the council was confronted by more than two hundred people who assembled to protest the island. Recognizing the need for further discussion, as well as the need for a larger forum, the council scheduled an "Ocean Front Revitalization" public hearing at the Santa Monica Civic Auditorium on January 23.

One thousand people filled the auditorium to protest the island that night, voices that carried the meeting

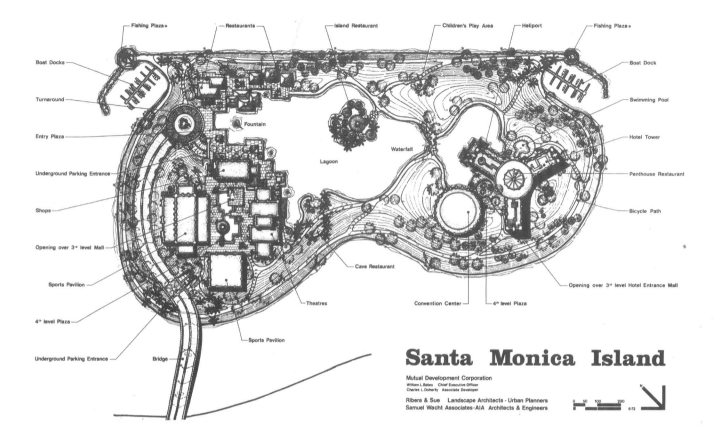

Santa Monica Island labels (clockwise from top left): Fishing Plaza, Restaurants, Island Restaurant, Children's Play Area, Heliport, Fishing Plaza, Boat Docks, Boat Dock, Turnaround, Swimming Pool, Entry Plaza, Hotel Tower, Underground Parking Entrance, Fountain, Penthouse Restaurant, Shops, Waterfall, Lagoon, Bicycle Path, Opening over 3rd level Mall, Sports Pavilion, Cave Restaurant, Opening over 3rd level Hotel Entrance Mall, 4th level Plaza, Theatres, Convention Center, 4th level Plaza, Underground Parking Entrance, Bridge, Sports Pavilion

Santa Monica Island

Mutual Development Corporation
William L. Bates   Chief Executive Officer
Charles L. Doherty   Associate Developer

Ribera & Sue   Landscape Architects - Urban Planners
Samuel Wacht Associates-AIA   Architects & Engineers

0   50   100   200

6-72

Plans for the proposed Santa Monica Island.

until well after midnight. The council heeded their protest, and voted to disapprove the island project. As the jubilant crowd left the building commending each other on their success, a murmur began to emanate from those who had remained in the chambers. The rumbling sound became clearer as it reached the people outside the auditorium, escalating finally to the cries of "They're going to tear down the pier!" Only minutes after the defeat of the island project, while most public ears had turned away from the dais, the council abruptly passed a motion to destroy both the Municipal and Newcomb Piers.

The stunned community immediately took action. Two citizens' groups, *Friends of the Santa Monica Pier* and the *Save Santa Monica Pier Citizens' Committee*, promptly formed and set forth to sway public opinion against destroying the pier. Each group embarked upon grassroots publicity campaigns, circulating flyers, buttons, t-shirts, and bumper stickers, and soliciting support from Los An-

geles media to bring greater attention to the impending loss of the beloved pier. *Friends of the Santa Monica Pier* was a group of local artists and activists who based their operations in the small café, Al's Kitchen. The committee was chaired by cook Larry Barber and financed by owner Joan Crowne, but the mastermind behind it all was café manager Jack Sikking. According to Barber, "Sikking had the idea and the vision for what we might be able to do. He was a great resource with creative ideas." As the campaign gained momentum, Sikking developed a proposal to make the pier more economically viable and attractive. The *Save Santa Monica Pier Citizens' Committee*, co-chaired by Diana Cherman, Gary Sansing, and Leonard Clunes, congregated in the Sinbad's building. They worked closely with pier merchants and circulated a petition to save the pier. Signatures accumulated rapidly and easily.

Left: The "Save the Pier Citizens Committee Petition" page, featuring signatures from Hollywood icons Paul Newman and Robert Redford (marked by X's). Center: The front page of the Al's Kitchen restaurant menu, early 1973. Food items were on subsequent pages, with more pressing matters presented on the front. Right: The Santa Monica Municipal Pier was saved on February 27, 1973, but the section with most of the pier's businesses remained vulnerable to demolition.

When the city council met again on February 13, they were again greeted by a passionate crowd. An estimated 350 people filled the chambers and overflowed into the hallway; the chant "Save the Pier" echoed throughout the building. Councilman John McCloskey, who had previously voted against demolishing the piers, proposed a motion to rescind the council's decision; the motion was tabled. Members of the public demanded a public hearing; they were denied. Diana Cherman approached the dais with a thick stack of petitions signed by over ten thousand people; it was rejected. The public's frustration festered as each attempt to discuss saving the pier was rejected, and the room grew hot and uncomfortable. Sensing that emotions were about to erupt, Mayor Anthony Dituri appeased the crowd by allowing *Friends of the Santa Monica Pier* chair Larry Barber to speak. The crowd hushed as Barber detailed Jack Sikking's inspired plan to restore and revitalize the pier. The council and the audience were invited to visualize a completely renovated carousel, a mu-

seum, an art gallery, a theater, upscale restaurants, and a park. "The pier is a place of magic," Barber said, "It's a place to renew myself. That's why we come here with a plan not for urban renewal, but for human renewal." The presentation provided a glimpse of hope on an otherwise disheartening night, yet it did nothing to sway the council's decision. The meeting ended as it had begun; the pier's fate remained the same.

Undeterred, the campaign to save the pier shifted to another gear. Three of the city council's seats were up for reelection, and the incumbents who occupied those seats, Robert Gabriel, Arthur Rinck, and James Reidy, Jr., became public targets for their failure to support the pier. A massive campaign was undertaken to support candidates who wished to save the pier, and the three incumbents soon took notice. By the end of February, Gabriel, Rinck, and Reidy each announced that they had changed their stance about the demolition of the pier. At the next council meeting, February 27, 1973, the council

voted unanimously to rescind the order to demolish the Municipal Pier. The council took no action in regard to the Newcomb Pier, however. Since the Newcomb lease had expired, the order to raze it by November 1 still stood. The council then proposed a citizens' committee that would make recommendations for the best use of the beachfront and the pier.

The community was not satisfied. The Newcomb Pier was considered a vital and precious part of the pier as a whole. The Santa Monica Pier Businessmen's Association, though less visible in the early months of the Save the Pier campaign, emerged as the election came closer. Their slogan "Don't Disap-Pier" focused on making certain that the *whole* pier survived. The best way to ensure this was to continue with the plan to have Gabriel, Rinck, and Reidy removed from office.

The election of 1973 became a political turning point for Santa Monica. Long controlled by the wealthier community of businessmen and homeowners, the hotbed created by the Save the Pier movements initiated a youth

"Friends of the Santa Monica Pier" spokesperson Larry Barber addresses the city council, February 13, 1973.

movement in voter registration. As the polls closed on April 10, Gabriel, Rinck, and Reidy felt confident that they had been reelected. To their surprise, they were replaced by Fred Judson, Donna Swink, and Pieter van den Steenhoven.

The newly elected city council's first act was to decline renewal of City Manager Perry Scott's contract. The council then voted on May 8, 1973, to save the Newcomb Pier from its scheduled demolition. Then, after over a year of proposals, negotiations and legal filings, the city council negotiated the purchase of the amusement pier from Mrs. Newcomb Winslow on June 28, 1974, bringing ownership of both the Newcomb and Municipal Piers to the City of Santa Monica.

To ensure that the pier would never again be threatened by elected officials or any other interests, the "Citizens Initiative to Preserve the Piers" introduced Proposition 1, an initiative to preserve both the Municipal and (formerly) Newcomb Piers forever. The initiative passed by almost two-thirds of the vote on April 8, 1975. The Santa Monica Pier was not only saved, it was assured permanence. That year also saw the creation of the Santa Monica Landmarks Commission, initiated in part as a result of the "Save the Pier" campaign. On August 17, 1976, the Landmarks Commission honored the pier by declaring it an official historical landmark of the City of Santa Monica.

The pier still needed work—lots of it. Structural rehabilitation and business redevelopment were imperative if the pier was going to remain standing and become a viable contributor to the city. Caught up in the wave of optimism, numerous proposals for revitalizing the pier were introduced; a new amusement zone adjacent to the carousel was explored, restaurant entrepreneur Bob Morris presented plans to place his restaurant "Gladstone's 4 Fish" on the existing Fisherman's Wharf, and another group hoped to open a dance club inside the Bowling & Billiards Building. As the 1970s passed into the 1980s, however, each of these dreams faded away. In the fall of 1981, the City of Santa Monica created the Pier Task Force, a committee of people whose interests and talents were pooled to determine the development direction of the pier. The committee held a series of public meetings and workshops in order to gather public input to help determine their own recommendations. The pier's future now appropriately rested with the very people who had fought so fiercely to save it.

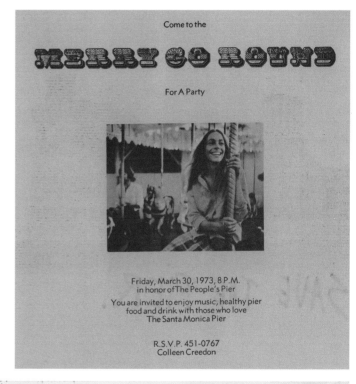

Below: Bumper stickers reminded drivers about the Santa Monica Pier. Right: Invitation to a "Save the Pier" party inside the pier's Merry-Go-Round building.

The atmosphere surrounding the Merry-Go-Round building has always had a nostalgic, romantic appeal.

Movie Stardom & Television Favorites

Ever since the advent of the motion picture industry in the early 1900s, the pier has been a regular sight on the big screen, securing its renown as the "World Famous Santa Monica Pier." Its relationship with the movie industry is unique. At times it has stretched beyond the camera/set dynamic into something even more interactive. Well-known actors have become trained as lifeguards, starting with Johnny Mack Brown, and including two famous Olympic-stars-turned-screen-performers, Buster Crabbe and Johnny Weissmuller. Weissmuller made headlines twice for performing rescues from the pier. An entire fleet of fully rigged sailing ships was moored in the yacht harbor for a short period in 1939 solely for use in Hollywood movies. The harbor became a venue for companies to develop techniques in underwater photography, and the lifeguards' aquarium shared a similar role with film companies who attempted to train ocean wildlife for the camera.

Among the multitudes of television shows that have had memorable moments on the pier are favorites such as *Charlie's Angels*, *TJ Hooker*, *Three's Company*, *24*, *Ugly Betty*, *CHiPs*, *Simon & Simon*, *Baywatch*, and *Modern Family*.

Movies often spend a considerable amount of time and attention on the pier's detail including 1965's *Inside Daisy Clover*, which shows extraordinary footage of the Newcomb Pier; 1961's *Night Tide*, in which Dennis Hopper takes the audience on a fantastic tour of the carousel building's apartments; and 2004's *Cellular*, which was shot extensively both on the pier and amid the pilings below deck. A short list of films shot at the pier includes:

A Society Sensation (1918), *Quicksand* (1950), *The Glenn Miller Story* (1953), *Elmer Gantry* (1960), *Funny Girl* (1968), *They Shoot Horses Don't They?* (1969), *The Sting* (1973), *Ruthless People* (1986), *Forrest Gump* (1994), *The Net* (1995), *The Majestic* (2001), *Cellular* (2004), *Fat Albert* (2004), *Bedtime Stories* (2008).

A film crew prepares for a beach shot, 1920s. Opposite: Actor Paul Nemman leans on fellow-actor Robert Redford for a quick word while preparing for a scene in the 1973 film, *The Sting*.

Top: Robert Redford and Eileen Brennan in *The Sting*. Below Left: Peter Lorre and Mickey Rooney in *Quicksand* (1950). Below Right: Dennis Hopper and Luana Anders in *Night Tide* (1961).

Left: Natalie Wood runs on the pier in the film *Inside Daisy Clover* (1965). Right: A scene from the animated show *Rocket Power.*

The earliest of these, *A Society Sensation*, was a silent film starring the famous ladies' man Rudolph Valentino opposite actress Carmel Myers. One scene, shot under the pier, called for Myers to be in the water, fully dressed and in need of rescuing. Director Paul Power repeatedly yelled for Valentino to jump in and save her—the scripted action in the scene. Valentino continually ignored the order. Finally, after holding up production for quite some time, Valentino jumped into the water to satisfy the director. At that moment, just after he had done his director's bidding, it was revealed that Valentino couldn't swim. He sank, and had to be rescued.

The movie most associated with the pier is the 1973 classic, *The Sting.* Fittingly, the stories surrounding this classic film are now firmly part of the pier's proud lore. The movie was filmed during the tumultuous period when the pier was under the threat of being torn down. While people outside the movie set were working hard to save the pier, the film crew and its stars, Robert Redford and Paul Newman, were concentrating on creating the atmosphere of Depression-era Chicago. Desperately in need of a break in the tension, each of the famous actors eagerly complied.

Jay Kennedy, an off-duty Los Angeles police officer working security for the film, recalls lighthearted moments with each of the film's famous stars. While New-man was preparing for a scene shot inside the carousel building, he spotted Kennedy eating fish and chips. Just as director George Roy Hill called "Action!," Newman grabbed a handful of the security guard's lunch, shoved it into his mouth, and turned toward the camera with a mouthful of food, forcing Hill to stop shooting. Hill gave Newman a few minutes to finish chewing, then, just as they were ready to start filming again, Newman put another handful of food in his mouth and turned to the camera again—mouth full and unable to do his lines. As for Redford, he enjoyed throwing a football. "He'd finish shooting a scene," Kennedy recalls, "come nudge me with the ball, and we'd go off and play catch. That's all he wanted to do!"

The threat of losing the Santa Monica Pier did not escape the two high-profile actors' attention. Both Redford and Newman, each known to be press shy, took time to pose for photos and share their feelings of support for saving the pier. The Santa Monica-born and raised Redford, in an interview with the *Los Angeles Times*, stated "The pier is a landmark. Everybody likes to visit the pier. I think it should be made into a museum. Not just out of nostalgia, but for a sense of history." Both men even signed the petition to save the pier. Those signed petitions were in turn presented to the city council and the pier was indeed saved.

The mysterious and fascinating underside of the Santa Monica Pier. The extra light comes from missing deck boards, which were being replaced.

6

THE STORMS OF 1983

*F*or nearly three-quarters of a century, the pier stood fast against any attempts to dismantle it. When its original concrete piles succumbed to the erosive power of nature, the pier persevered; its pilings replaced while the deck still hovered above the sea. Storms raged, then passed, but the pier carried on. When progress threatened to cast it aside, the people stood by it and assured it infinite life. In the early months of 1983, just under a decade after being preserved by the people, the pier's resilience finally failed. Neptune, so long defeated by the sturdy pier, finally had his revenge.

The volatile storm season was no surprise to Santa Monicans; in fact, many thought the area was due—the "Hundred Years' Storm," some called it. Scientists predicted that the warm waters associated with the "El Nino" phenomenon would profoundly affect the winter of 1982-83.

The 1983 storms effectively ended all public vehicle access to the west end of the pier. Opposite: El Niño made a strong statement during the winter of 1983, destroying many of southern California's piers and severely damaging the Santa Monica Pier.

Cocktail napkins from Moby's Dock and Sinbad's; Both businesses were under the same ownership but only Moby's Dock lasted to see these catastrophic storms. Sinbad's, visible in the photo opposite, had been closed and vacant for ten years by the time the pier's revered lower fishing deck at its west end was destroyed by a storm on January 27, 1983.

But no one anticipated the power of El Nino's storms. During the last week of January, Southern California was battered by four of them.

On the morning of January 27, 1983, the third and most powerful storm struck the pier. Swells were predicted to reach ten feet and, since the lower fishing deck of the pier stood only about eight feet above the water, some part of the pier inevitably was going to give way. The news of the impending drama spread quickly. Crowds braved a brutal and driving rain as they lined up along the cliffs of Palisades Park to witness nature's fury. Shortly after dawn, waves broke over the top of the fishing deck and, within less than two hours, most of the lower deck washed away. The northwest corner separated from the rest of the pier, stood solitarily for a moment, and then plunged into the water.

The lifeguard station was the first victim, followed by the Oatman Rock Shop, the Porthole Café, and the boat lockers. Maintenance workers who had been observing the storm from the precarious west end realized that they were in danger and hurried toward safety at the shore end. The Santa Monica Police Department barred access to the entire west end. By 9:30 a.m., the Harbormaster's Office, too, was lost. Only Santa Monica Sportfishing and the lifeguard boat *Santa C* remained atop the west end deck.

As the storm subsided, people flocked to the beach south of the pier to collect souvenirs—pieces of the pier washed ashore, littering the area with shards, splinters, and entire sections of the once-proud wooden structure. Others stood silently, observing the wreckage in solemn despair. With another storm approaching, the city closed the pier and the beach until public safety could be assured.

City engineers surveyed the damage and determined that the pier was not as severely damaged as early indications had led them to believe. It hardly mattered what they said, however—there was little argument as to whether or not the pier would be saved. "The overwhelming sense of the community is to fully restore the pier," City Manager John Alschuler told the *Los Angeles Times*.

Reconstruction commenced within a couple of weeks. A thirty-ton crane was brought onto the pier to begin the process of demolishing the dangerous remains of the lower deck.

The harsh "El Nino" season was not over yet, though. A new, more powerful storm teamed up with the year's highest tides to take advantage of the reeling pier. Upon hearing weather reports issued by the United States Coast Guard, the city's pier maintenance officials warned the construction crew that the crane needed to be moved to a more stable part of the pier. The crew moved the crane about fifty feet shoreward, but with the workday ending soon and the hard rains increasing, the crew stopped and pronounced it safe at its new location. At about 8:30 p.m. on March 1, 1983, the pier began to sway with the powerful surf. Sections fell off the west end and, as midnight approached, the pilings underneath the heavy crane collapsed, sending the crane tumbling into the sea.

THE STORMS OF 1983

SANTA MONICA PIER

The crane began knocking over the pilings within its immediate vicinity while the large timbers that had supported it drifted into the Newcomb Pier. Within fifteen minutes, the entire west end of the Municipal Pier was destroyed, sending more timber toward the Newcomb Pier. Pilings collapsed under Moby's Dock and the Newcomb parking lot. Three cars and a refrigeration truck toppled into the sea. Debris, stacked ten feet high in some places, was once again scattered along the coast south of the pier. By midmorning on March 2, the storm relented, having taken about one-third of the pier's square footage with it—an estimated $6.4 million worth of damage.

The Santa Monica Pier was not the only victim of the March 1 storm. Piers at Seal Beach, Mission Beach, and Malibu's Paradise Cove were demolished as well. The sand surrounding the entrance to the concrete fishing pier in Venice washed away until it left the pier standing as somewhat of an island, inaccessible to the public. Presi-

dent Ronald Reagan toured the damaged Santa Monica Bay area via helicopter, noting the "devastation and the awesome power of the sea."

While the council had voted to quickly restore the pier after the first storm, the damage inflicted by the second was so devastating that the city acknowledged the process now would be much more difficult, time consuming, and expensive. Crews immediately began cleaning up the pier and shoring it up with new pilings in damaged areas, but the project of rebuilding the western sections of both the Newcomb and Municipal Piers would have to wade through the bureaucratic process.

Deck boards and other debris washed up onto the beach south of the pier after the January 27 storm. Opposite: The remnants of the historic Santa Monica Pier after damage from the March 1, 1983 storm.

The severely beaten west end of the pier hangs precariously above the ocean after the highly destructive January 27 storm.

The Pier in Pop Culture

The Santa Monica Pier inspired artists of all genres, including painters, photographers, authors, poets, and musicians. Murals throughout the Los Angeles area decorate large wall spaces to commemorate the pier's place in the world. Paintings and photographs of the pier grace art galleries as well as people's homes and workplace, transporting the viewer to the splendor of the pier, even if just for a fanciful moment.

Literary works, both fiction and nonfiction, have staged significant parts of their stories on the century-old structure. Raymond Chandler's noir mystery *Farewell My Lovely* portrays a subversive side of Santa Monica and its pier, inspired by the mob-operated gambling ships that were serviced by water taxis based at the pier. Nancy Boyarsky, a contemporary mystery novelist, stages a murder below the pier, juxtaposing a dark and perilous world below the fun and frivolity of the amusement park above. In the nonfiction genre, Carlotta Monti's *W.C. Fields & Me* highlights Mr. Fields' friendship with a longtime Philadelphian friend who took up quarters in the apartments above the pier's merry-go-round.

Inspiration is found everywhere on the pier, seen here in the painting *Harbor Entrance* by Tom Brittain. Opposite, Top: the long-beloved Santa Monica mural *Unbridled* by David Gordon. Opposite, Bottom: the photograph *Colorful Umbrellas* Tom Lackey.

Likewise poets—amateur and renowned alike—have used the pier as their subject. One of the most notable poets was Charles Bukowski, whose edgy style brought him both praise and disparagement throughout the latter half of the twentieth century. For a time in the early 1970s, Bukowski visited the pier regularly and was rumored to be dating a woman who lived in an apartment above the merry-go-round. His time there is reflected in three poems: "The Fisherman," "The Catch," and "Save the Pier." "Save the Pier," recounts the real-life grassroots community fight to save the pier from demolition. The following are the opening lines as published in *Burning in Water, Drowning in Flame (Selected Poems 1955–1973)*:

SAVE THE PIER
You shoulda been at this party,
I know you hate parties
But you seem to be at most of them.
Anyhow, I took my girl, you know
Her —
Java Jane?
Yes, this party was at the merry-go-round
Where they are trying to tear the pier down, you
Know where that is?
Yes, the red paint, the broken
Windows —
Yes, anyhow, my girl lives in a room just above the
Merry-go-round. It's a
Birthday party for the woman who owns the
Merry-go-round.
She's trying to save the pier
She's trying to save the merry-go-round —
Plenty of drinks for everybody, my girl lives in the
Room right above the
Merry-go-round.
Sounds great.

And, naturally, some poetry about the pier has been put to music, perhaps most notably the Tommy Mack-penned 1948 song "When Veronica Plays the Harmonica (on the Pier at Santa Monica)," recorded by Kay Kyser's Campus Cowboys. The fun, jazzy tune tells the tale of a woman whose harmonica-playing abilities draw sea creatures of every kind to the pier, just to enjoy her songs. In 1968, actor/singer Noel Harrison (son of actor Rex Harri-son) recorded an album titled *Santa Monica Pier*, featuring a lively folk tune by the same name. And in 1988, artist Christine Lavin wrote and sang her own Santa Monica Pier song. While each of these songs never reached a high position on the popularity charts, it is clear what their inspiration was, and that inspiration continues today as you can often hear a busker on the pier mentioning the iconic structure in one of their original songs.

7 RESTORATION

*I*n the wake of the 1983 storms, the pier was nearly forgotten. For many, the entire pier had disappeared and was quickly becoming an afterthought—just a few pages in a history book. The city council knew that was a dangerous misconception. So it focused instead on raising public awareness that there was still a pier in Santa Monica. The council designated a week in late May as Save the Pier Week and established a committee to produce corresponding events. The Save the Pier Week extravaganza opened on May 23, 1983, with a parade of Arabian horses, presentations by city officials, and a series of jazz, reggae, and country/rock concerts throughout the day. Festivities continued throughout the week, including art exhibits, a crafts fair, street performers, and enjoyable competitions including a pie-eating contest, a "cutest baby" contest, and a pier-building contest. Dances were held in the

OPENING CEREMONIES
CAROUSEL PARK
Santa Monica Pier
Friday, June 6, 1986, 4 P.M.

Program from the opening ceremony of Carousel Park, part of the Santa Monica Pier's multi-year revitalization and restoration effort. Opposite: Santa Monica Pier in the mid-1980s. After the devastating 1983 storms, the pier persevered.

big blue-and-white La Monica Tent, and concerts thrilled crowds every night, culminating in a Friday night show with performances by rock 'n' roll stars Ry Cooder and Christine McVie. A Sunday night film tribute featured movies filmed on the pier: *Inside Daisy Clover*, *The Sting,* and *Elmer Gantry.*

In September 1983, the council made inaugural appointments to the Pier Restoration Corporation (PRC) board of directors, and the new board held its first meeting a few weeks later. Continuing with the goals set forth by the Pier Task Force prior to the storms, the PRC proceeded with plans to finance, design, and ultimately, rebuild the pier. Guidelines were established that would maintain the unique character of the pier, while also exploring how to bring in enough revenue to support its operations.

In the spring of 1985, the PRC presented the public with two proposed plans for the new pier. One proposal called for a $10.2 million wooden and concrete pier ex-

Left: Independence Day fireworks show off of the west end of the pier, early 1980s. Bottom: The pier's desolate main walkway after a rainstorm, 1980s.

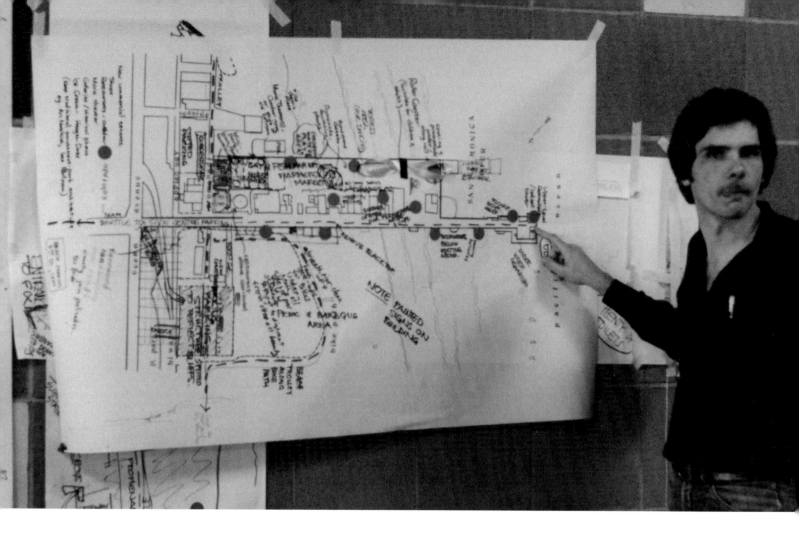

Pier Task Force member Darrell Clarke in a 1985 community workshop.

tending directly from the point where the pier then ended. The project would take about six to eight months to complete, and would include a protective breakwater to be reconstructed and extended three hundred feet southward. The other called for an $11.3 million all-concrete pier and concrete lower deck. Many of the Municipal Pier's surviving wooden pilings would be removed and replaced with concrete piles. This rebuilt version would take eight to ten months to construct yet was considered strong enough to withstand storms without the aid of a breakwater. If the accompanying concrete lower deck were to succumb to a storm it would immediately sink to the ocean floor, rather than crash into the pier's pilings as had happened in 1983. In addition, maintenance costs associated with an all-concrete pier were estimated to be far less than the

combination wooden and concrete proposal. The public response was in favor of the all-concrete pier.

When the PRC proposed the all-concrete plan to the city council in May 1985, the city attorney voiced concern that the plans might be in violation of the Save the Pier ordinance passed in 1975, which stated that major alterations required a majority vote of the people. The council settled on a compromise plan that would use concrete pilings extending from the pier's current end and leave the existing structure standing on its wooden piles. The lower deck at the end of the pier would still be

composed of concrete. The plans passed unanimously on May 21, 1985, and construction was slated to begin in the late spring of 1986.

Drawing on the positive experience of Save the Pier Week, the city's arts commission enlisted producer Katharine King to organize a series of free concerts in June of 1985. Established as a tribute to the La Monica Ballroom, the series was an instant success and evolved into the extraordinarily popular Twilight Dance Series.

On June 6, 1986, the newly remodeled east end of

the pier opened. The new grand entrance and carousel park, designed by the Santa Monica-based architectural firm Campbell & Campbell, added new life to what had long been a dismal part of the pier's surroundings. The grand entrance recalled the tiered effect of the original Looff picnic pavilion and invited people up onto the new deck outside the historic carousel building. The park,

with its giant stone dragon head and Viking-style boat, recalled mythical legends of sailing ships and sea monsters, providing children an outdoor playground. Temporary carnival rides, set up in the pier parking lot, accompanied the opening of the park, and were so popular that they were set up annually for the next decade.

Fourth of July firework celebrations, a beach tradition since Santa Monica's earliest days, continued to be a huge draw into the latter decades of the twentieth century. Both the pier and the surrounding beaches were annually inundated with people, but, by the 1980s, incidents of violence were on the rise. On July 4, 1986, the final nighttime fireworks show at the pier took place. A new approach was taken in 1987, when the city introduced "Dawn's Early Light"—a fireworks celebration that began at 4 a.m. on the holiday. The early morning concept reduced neither the crowds nor the violence. In fact, most people stayed at the pier all night prior to the morning show, many of them intoxicated. Reports of violence, drunk driving, and mayhem actually increased. And overcast early-morning skies often led to disappointing visual shows. The rising cost of these events, when compared to the growing list of problems related to them, brought the city to an inevitable and unpopular decision. After the 1990 celebration, the city announced that Fourth of July fireworks at the pier would cease, a huge disappointment to the local community.

In November 1987, the Kiewit Pacific Company began reconstruction of the pier and progressed quickly. The Newcomb Pier was complete by August 1988, and the new west end's finishing touches were being applied as 1990 approached. Fishing decks were built on both the north and south sides of the new pier and a large, thirteen foot-wide lower deck wrapped around the north and west sides at the pier's end.

On April 6, 1990, the new west end opened to the public for the first time. Mayor Dennis Zane presided over the opening day ceremonies and Joan Crowne, former owner of Al's Kitchen who had mortgaged her home in order to help save the pier in 1973, was awarded the first-ever Santa Monica Pier Prize. The new west end was overwhelmingly well received and the pier, as well as the rest of Santa Monica, felt whole again.

The people most ecstatic about the completion of the west end were the fishermen and fisherwomen. Robert Khourney made the first official catch off the new pier—a white sea bass. Staying true to the spirit of the old pier's history, though, the first fish were actually caught prior to the pier's opening day. John "Yosh" Volaski, a pier maintenance worker at the time, snuck out onto the end of the pier during the night before opening day and "unofficially" hauled in several sea bass.

In 1991, that very same fisherman, Yosh Volaski, opened Santa Monica Bait & Tackle Shop, the first new business at the west end. For Volaski, it was the crowning achievement of a lifetime spent on the pier. As a young boy, he frequently skipped school, followed the Red Line railway tracks to the pier, and fished all day. Finding a way to spend his working days on his beloved pier, he found work on fishing boats, in bait shops, and ultimately, with the city's pier maintenance crew. When he got the chance to bid on the ownership of the new bait-and-tackle shop at the west end of the pier, it was as if he'd heard his calling.

As the new pier took shape, the PRC was confronted with how best to develop and operate the city's landmark. The need to maintain the pier's traditions while becoming self-sufficient was the topic of endless discussion; the prevailing sentiment was that the pier should function as a park—accessible to all people, all of the time.

By the time the new west end opened, Moby's Dock and the Shooting Gallery had been razed and Skipper's, a fast food restaurant on the northwest corner of the carousel, had been evicted. The Crown and Anchor, an English pub-style restaurant that occupied the former Fish 'n' Chips space, was struggling, and many of the operators on the pier had begun to worry for their future. The Sinbad's building, hailed as a landmark and considered vital to the pier's profile, yet so decayed that it was hazardous—was demolished in April of 1993. Rumors circulated that major development and corresponding high rents were on the horizon.

The PRC, recognizing that this pier was the last remnant of an atmosphere that once defined Santa Monica, turned its focus to bringing back the amusement atmosphere that had delighted crowds for so many generations.

Left: Aerial view of the original Cirque du Soleil tents next to the pier. Right: The cast of the original touring Cirque du Soleil production.

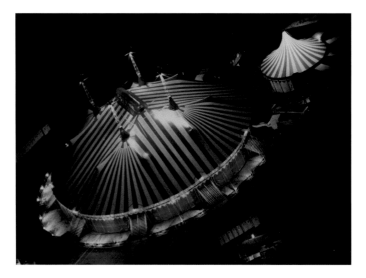

While some locals were resistant to change, recreating a pier reminiscent of its earliest days while updating it with new restaurants, rides, and attractions seemed the most sensible and profitable direction to go. The PRC set forth on finding a suitable company to bring an amusement park to the pier.

In the summer of 1994, the restaurant/nightclub Rusty's Surf Ranch replaced the defunct Crown and Anchor. Owner Russell Barnard, guided by the same nostalgic sense that was encompassing the pier, reestablished pocket billiards in the old Bowling & Billiards Building for the first time in over fifty years. Weekly pool tournaments at Rusty's revived the spirit of old "Pop" Kerns and even drew the interest of professional players like international trick-pool champion Mike Massey. With live

Main entrance to Pacific Park, the Santa Monica Pier's first full-time amusement park since 1930.

music a regular part of its program, Rusty's became a mainstay on the pier with notable performances by nationally known acts such as Bonnie Raitt adding to an already popular schedule of local acts, like the Red Elvises.

In the summer of 1995, Mariasol Cocina joined the Harbor Patrol and Santa Monica Pier Bait & Tackle at the west end, delivering the nostalgic aroma of hot food on the grill wafting across the entire pier.

On May 25, 1996, Pacific Park opened its rides to the public, establishing the first permanent, full-scale amusement park on the pier since 1930, and with it came both a sense of nostalgia and of renewed energy. The

opening of the amusement park was the first and greatest step toward reshaping the pier's reputation into an all-ages, family friendly venue.

The quickly changing face of the new pier was not without its victims. The longtime midway games and bumper cars that helped define the pier experience for decades gave way to the more sophisticated Pacific Park, which included the same amenities but with a different, albeit upgraded, flair. Doreena the fortuneteller, a fixture on the pier since the 1940s, lost her space on the pier, but she and her family managed to stay nearby in a new location on Ocean Front Walk, just east of the carousel for several years.

The pier's history was honored in another reincarnation in 1996—this time under the deck east of the carousel. The University of California, Los Angeles opened the UCLA Ocean Discovery Center—an aquarium aimed toward educating the public, particularly children, about the ocean life found in Santa Monica Bay, much like Cap Watkins and his lifeguards proudly displayed next to their office in the La Monica Ballroom. In 2003, Heal the Bay assumed the operations of the aquarium, establishing a site under the pier where school groups and the general public can get up-close views of local fish such as the California halibut, sarcastic fringehead, and kelp bass. Interactive tanks are also available in which patrons can touch sharks, starfish, and numerous other creatures found in the bay.

The Boathouse, after thirty-five years on the pier, also found itself out of place in the pier's new atmosphere. During negotiations for a new lease, the city demanded major changes, including a cap on liquor sales, installation of a public elevator, and improvements to the dilapidated structure. Boathouse ownership resisted, citing the expense of the elevator and extensive remodeling as unacceptable. In 2001, the city awarded the lease for the Boathouse property to the Bubba Gump Shrimp

Pacific Park's West Coaster roller coaster and Pacific Wheel hover above the Pacific Ocean.

Company, a chain owned by Paramount Pictures Corporation. The community was outraged. Throughout the pier's life it had remained free of corporate-owned chains, yet the city was forcing out a family-run restaurant in favor of a corporate chain. Letters filled the local newspapers and angry citizens filled the city council chambers, reminiscent of the days three decades earlier when the fate of the pier was at stake. This time, however, the protests failed. The Boathouse was evicted.

The pier's quick growth and upgrading did have the potential to invite corporate interests that would destroy the character and flavor of the pier. Chain restaurants had already found their way into Pacific Park, seemingly overnight. The PRC set language within the pier's leasing guidelines that discouraged the city from leasing to corporate chains.

Bubba Gump Shrimp Company opened its doors in November 2005. The newly rebuilt structure carefully resembles the restaurant it replaced. But, when customers walk through the establishment's front doors, instead of the sound of live music and the smell of stale beer, they immediately encounter an image of actor Tom Hanks jogging to the end of the pier in the film *Forrest Gump*, homage to the pier's longtime role as a movie star in its own right.

As the pier changed, so too did the natural environment around it. For decades the railings along the pier supported signs advising people not to eat White Croaker, if caught, for the species had been identified as having high DDT contaminant levels. Those signs were removed in the early 2000s as the contaminant danger substantially subsided. As DDT levels decreased, brown pelicans began frequenting the Santa Monica Pier and beach area, a clear indication that their status as an endangered species was much improved.

In the spring of 2008, the New York Trapeze School assumed the space left vacant by the Sinbad's building fifteen years prior. The sight of the experienced and inexperienced flying through the air added to the whimsy on the pier, as did the daily presence of street performers. For many years, the city discouraged the presence of musicians and artists who performed in front of an open hat, but, in 2001, the city drafted an ordinance that allowed for fair and organized street performance. The city council reasoned that the pier, especially with its new amusement park, was a natural location for these artists and entertainers. Since the inception of this ordinance, the pier has hosted mimes, tarot card readers, painters,

Left: Postcard depicting the popular Boathouse restaurant in the 1980s. Right: A salmon-colored moon crowns Bubba Gump Shrimp Company, which replaced the Boathouse restaurant in 2005.

calligraphers, acrobats, musicians, and many other street performers. The most popular among these buskers, Tim "Bubbleman" Dillenbeck, has become so regularly associated with his bubble-making performances on the carousel deck that he is one of the pier's featured attractions. His bubbles are said to have drifted as far as five miles away.

Encouraged by the success of the long-running Twilight Dance Series, the PRC focused on hosting more large-scale events on the expansive parking lot on the pier. Organizations such as the Special Olympics of Southern California found the space to be perfect for annual fundraisers, while corporate and promotional events delighted in the unique and fanciful beachfront atmosphere.

Beginning in September 2008, the pier enjoyed a year-long celebration of its first 100 years with events including an homage to the glory days of the La Monica Ballroom, a day full of circus acts to celebrate the pier's eclectic nature, an all-star Twilight Dance Series that featured legendary folk musician Joan Baez, culminating with a fireworks extravaganza on September 9, 2009—the official 100th anniversary of the pier's opening day.

Left: One of the many midway games in the pier's Fun Zone, which attracted visitors to the pier from the 1970s through the mid-1990s. Right: Pacific Park replaced the Fun Zone in 1996 with high-impact rides, including the West Coaster roller coaster.

In June 2010, the PRC introduced a new annual event of its own, the Santa Monica Pier Paddleboard Race and Ocean Festival, to kick off the summer season with races featuring the burgeoning new sport of stand-up paddleboarding. The event proved a natural fit for the pier, and in subsequent years other beach and water sports, such as beach volleyball and swim events, were added. In 2018, the name was changed to the Pier 360 Beach Festival.

The completion of the pier's restoration and reimagination was officially in March 2012 when Santa Monica city officials removed "restoration" from the Santa Monica Pier Restoration Corporation shortening its title to Santa Monica Pier Corporation. The city continued to shore up parts of the pier with significant reconstruction projects, but the overall status of the iconic structure was clear: the Santa Monica Pier was officially restored.

The pier continued to be infused with new energy, consistent with its perpetual growth in popularity. By 2012, the annual number of visitors was estimated to exceed ten million people, a 500% increase from estimates prior to the restoration. With the new energy came continued change, particularly with the restaurant offerings. Inside the merry-go-round building, a new "old-fashioned" ice cream soda fountain called Soda Jerks was introduced in 2010. In the middle of the pier, longtime seafood restaurant Surf View Café was replaced in 2011 by Pier Burger—the first foray into fast food by the

highly successful fine dining company King's Seafood. The following year, the family ownership of Santa Monica Pier Seafood passed from one generation to the next and, along with it, a complete rebranding was undertaken. With a new menu and atmosphere came a new name, The Albright. In 2013, a long-vacant space next to the pier's merry-go-round building was occupied by Ristorante Al Mare, an Italian-inspired seafood restaurant that ambitiously expanded skyward with rooftop dining. Al Mare's time on the pier was short-lived, though, and, in 2018, new owner Robert Earl (of Planet Hollywood fame) introduced it as Seaside on the Pier.

The late winter of 2020 brought a new harsh reality, however, with the emergence of the COVID-19 pandemic. On March 16, 2020, the State of California ordered a closure of entertainment destinations and the population was ordered to begin social-distancing during what quickly became a nationwide, ultimately worldwide, pandemic. The pier had experienced closures before, but rarely for more than a day and never for more than a few days. As the Los Angeles region began to reopen on May 8 that year, the pier was restricted from reopening due to its status as a gathering place, since social distancing remained a priority. Making a bad situation even worse, the civil unrest that had been spreading throughout the United States after the murder of George Floyd reached downtown Santa Monica on May 31. By an odd stroke of good fortune, the pier was still closed due to the pandemic, and the Santa Monica Police Department prevented anyone from accessing the pier. In the following days, the United States National Guard was brought in to secure parts of Santa Monica, including the pier, marking only the second time the pier had to be secured by federal troops (the first was in the aftermath of the 1992 Rodney King unrest).

Finally, on June 24, 2020, the pier reopened for public visitation, albeit in limited function. Restaurants were only allowed to reopen their outdoor facilities, with the city granting them space extended from their normal footprints. Pacific Park, like other amusement parks throughout California, remained closed until April 2, 2021.

As concerns following the pandemic subsided, the pier quickly regained its status as a highly enjoyable outdoor venue, solidifying its status as an enduring American icon.

Left and Center: The COVID-19 pandemic had a dramatic impact on the pier, forcing a three-and-a-half month closure in 2020. Even after reopening, visitors were required to wear protective masks and practice social distancing. Right: View of the pier from the mostly desolate beach south of the pier, spring 2020. Opposite: A sign commemorating the Santa Monica Pier's status as the celebrated end of historic Route 66.

The Twilight Dance Series

The success of 1983's Save the Pier Week caused an eye-popping realization: the Santa Monica Pier is a great concert venue. Katharine King, the woman responsible for the entertainment during Save the Pier Week, recognized the potential immediately. Not since the glory days of the La Monica Ballroom had the pier hosted regular concerts, and King decided to regenerate the excitement of those days with current, unique entertainers. The next year, King assembled another free concert series, this one running for four weeks in the middle of summer. The city took notice of the series' popularity, and, in 1985, the Santa Monica Arts Commission budgeted seven thousand dollars for King to produce a free event that would allow dancing on the pier. What she created was a concert/dance series that ran for seven weeks throughout the summer.

King determined that the shows should be scheduled during its most magnificent time of day—sunset. She considered Thursday nights to be ideal because they were "almost the weekend," increasing the likelihood that the public would come to enjoy a weeknight out with only one more work day ahead. Upon assembling it all, she named the series the "First Annual Santa Monica Twilight Dance Series." A summertime tradition was born.

For the first four years, King managed to provide exceptional shows on a minimal budget. An established producer/promoter before the inception of the series, King was able to rely on professional friendships, bringing in quality acts such as Poncho Sanchez and the Rhythm Kings, acts a limited budget wouldn't otherwise afford. In 1989, corporate sponsorships helped fund the series, enabling King to afford acts such as Bo Diddley and Los Lobos. The series quickly developed a reputation for mixing lesser-known international acts with classics in the musical world. Such an eclectic mix helped the series grow into the premier event in Santa Monica as well as one of the longest lasting, free concert series in Southern California.

As part of the year-long Santa Monica Pier Centennial Celebration, an all-star lineup was assembled for the 2009 season, which was also the twenty-fifth year of the series. The season featured longtime marquee acts such as Joan Baez and Patti Smith alongside the newly popular artist assemblage called the "Playing for Change" band. A tribute to the pier's past was also included, featuring "La Monica Revisited," an homage to the big bands that used to entertain patrons of the old La Monica Ballroom.

With the close of the 2010 season came a change in production companies for the series. With the change came a new brand name, the Twilight Concert Series, and a new programming direction that placed greater emphasis on acts that would draw more people. Crowds grew such that the pier deck could not contain all who attended, and the beach immediately adjacent to the pier became the primary gathering spot. At its peak, the concert series drew well over twenty thousand people, with the highest estimate reaching 22,000 for a new artist named Khalid on June 22, 2017.

The vast crowds—particularly on the beach—drew concerns about public safety from City of Santa Monica officials. While producers and city officials worked together in efforts to control crowd size and properly planned safety measures, the possibility of a public tragedy and how to mitigate it, particularly on the sand, remained prominent in safety officials' minds. With the high number of attendees in 2017, the future of the concerts were already in question. After the October 2, 2017 mass shooting tragedy at a Las Vegas music festival, the city and pier officials realized they had to either completely reimagine and downsize the series, or to cancel it altogether.

The two parties agreed to reimagine the series by moving the concert dates out of the summer season, moving show dates to Wednesdays instead of Thursdays, and booking lesser known, yet still high quality musical acts. For the 2018 and 2019 seasons, now renamed Twilight on the Pier, the series utilized the entirety of the pier as a venue by adding stages to the pier's west end and within the Pacific Park events pavilion. Large sculptures were placed along the main walkway of the pier, tying the three stage locations together with an art walk experience. For the 2019 season, comedy replaced music at the Pacific Park events pavilion stage. The changes had mixed results. The plan succeeded in that there were no longer large crowds gathering on the beach, and an added benefit was the sense of discovery of the entire pier as an event venue. The lower attendance, though, proved detrimental to the series as a whole, and as producers began planning for the 2020 season, the willingness of sponsors to pay for this much more modest series had severely waned. When the COVID-19 pandemic sent the world into quarantine, the prospect for a 2020 season (and then a 2021 season) suffered the same fate of all events. They would not happen. With the momentum of its thirty-five year run drawn to a standstill, the Twilight series came to a full and complete end.

8

TOURING THE PIER THROUGH TIME

*F*or over a century, the walk from beginning to end of the pier has been the same distance, save for the occasional storm damage or construction project, and for most of that time many of the buildings have also remained the same. But the memories, year-by-year, day-by-day, even minute-by-minute, are all completely unique to the individual. Still, there are some consistencies, for it would be difficult not to notice the fanciful old architecture of the merry-go-round building, or the bells and whistles of the arcade, or the towering and luminescent Ferris wheel at the amusement park, and not appreciate them in the same way as others. Those are today's constants. But have they always been there? And what are their stories? From beginning to end, shore to sea, the following is a historical tour of the Santa Monica Pier.

A brown pelican, nicknamed "Hemingway," perched atop the pier's harbor patrol all-terrain vehicle. Opposite: Color postcard of the pier depicting its 1920s La Monica Ballroom days.

The Famous Pier Sign

In 1939, work began on the Colorado Grade Separation Project, a complex highway project that was designed to improve access between the Pacific Coast Highway and city streets. The location of the project eliminated the traditional access to the pier, so planners designed a ramp at the end of Colorado Avenue to allow traffic to overpass the new access ways and travel directly onto the pier's deck.

Ground broke for the new pier ramp on September 19, 1939, closing the entrance to the Municipal Pier and tearing up part of the pier's east end. The city, recognizing that business would be severely hampered by the project, reduced rentals for businesses on the pier by 5 percent. Construction took five months and the ramp was opened for use on June 12, 1940.

The new access ramp was not clearly visible, nor was it obvious that it was indeed the correct route to the pier. This was of great concern to the businesses on the pier. With the money saved from the rent reduction during construction, the Santa Monica Pier Business Men's Association committed two thousand dollars to hire the Pan-Pacific Neon Sign Company to design and construct a neon sign and mount it at the top of the bridge. The now world-famous sign was unveiled on June 19, 1941 during a special ceremony in which it was formally presented to Santa Monica Mayor Claude C. Crawford and Commissioners D.C. Freeman and W.W. Milliken by the president of the Santa Monica Pier Business Men's Association, Dick Hernage. The ceremony was followed by a special photo session that resulted in the now-iconic image of the new sign hovering over a lineup of waving, smiling dignitaries composed of Santa Monica officials, pier business owners, and film actresses Martha O'Driscoll and Susan Hayward.

The arched blue sign—twenty feet at its highest point, twelve feet at its lowest, and supported by columns on each side of the ramp—has since become an internationally recognized icon. In 1996, the State of California Department of Parks and Recreation declared the sign a historic landmark. The official record notes its dual historical significance as: 1) a classic example of signage from the neon era, and 2) the designated marker for the last existing pleasure pier in an area in which they were once bountiful.

Advertising the pier as "Santa Monica Yacht Harbor," the sign's verbiage is a bit misleading today, but for the pier's old-timers it is a memory well worth preserving.

The "Santa Monica Yacht Harbor" sign. Opposite: Santa Monica commissioners and business owners pose alongside Hollywood actresses Susan Hayward (in a striped shirt) and Martha O'Driscoll (dressed in white) for the unveiling of the sign on June 19, 1941.

The Carousel & Hippodrome

On June 12, 1916, the Looff Hippodrome opened its doors to the public for the first time and the public fell in love, for inside the curious looking structure was a circling menagerie of wooden animals suited to delight anyone who cared to ride upon them. It was a genuine carousel. The music of an automatic band organ, manufactured by A. Ruth & Son of Waldkirch, Germany, accompanied the animals. The organ's sound could be heard well into the town, drawing people toward its melody and the stable of fun inside.

The Hippodrome, a mixture of Byzantine, Moorish, and California architecture, is a two-story structure measuring just over one hundred feet square. Its swooping roof and corner turrets give the building a whimsical allure. The second floor was built as both office and apartment space, housing the owners and management of the new pier's development project.

The carousel inside was a Looff original, hand-crafted by Charles Looff himself. It offered a mixture of hand-carved horses, giraffes, camels, tigers, and other jungle animals, all jumpers—animals that move up-and-down—spreading three rows across the revolving platform. Brass rings were dispensed, awarding free rides to the lucky recipients. The ride was so popular that, within three months of its first run, it was expanded to include an outer row of twenty-four additional animals. Surrounding the carousel were rocking chairs where non-riders could relax and watch the wooden animals and their passengers circle around.

The beloved antique 1922 Philadelphia Toboggan Company carousel inside the Looff Hippodrome is one of the most treasured attractions in the world.

In 1939, while the amusement pier struggled with ownership issues, the Looff carousel was sold to the Belmont Park amusement park in Mission Beach, San Diego. It remained there until 1976, when it was disassembled and sold off in pieces. A C.W. Parker #316 carousel, previously housed on the Ocean Park Pier, replaced the Looff unit. The Parker, made in Leavenworth, Kansas, in 1916, was originally built for use in a beer parlor, but the timing of Prohibition relegated it to storage for several years before it found a home on the Ocean Park Pier in 1925.

The Parker carousel remained in the Hippodrome until 1947, when Walter Newcomb sold it to make room for his own carousel, the Philadelphia Toboggan Company #62. Newcomb found it in the 1930s through a classified advertisement in *Showman's National Magazine*. He sent his brother Ted to inspect it, who then bought it on sight. He first installed the carousel on the Venice Pier, but when that pier burned in 1947, Newcomb moved it to its new home in the Hippodrome. The Philadelphia Toboggan Company #62 carousel remains there today as one among only a handful of historic, all-wooden merry-go-rounds in operation.

A standard Philadelphia Toboggan Carousel, its two interior rows consist entirely of jumpers, while the hors-es on the outer row are all standing. The noble animals number forty-four in all. Interspersed among them are two sleighs suitable for riders who prefer not to climb on a horse. The music accompanying the horses today alternates between recorded selections and those provided by an original Wurlitzer Model 146 Automatic Band Organ.

In 1954, George and Eugene Gordon assumed management of the carousel. The brothers eventually bought the business and upgraded the manual operated crank machinery to the more modern electrical system that exists today. They made only a few other changes during their ownership, the most significant being the removal of the brass ring dispenser in the early 1970s.

Longtime carousel operator Jockey Stevens not only worked in the carousel, he lived in one of the upstairs apartments. A quiet man with a weathered face, he assisted children and adults alike onto the horses, taking their coin fare and depositing it into his change belt. Perhaps his most memorable encounter, though, was with a

Left: The pier's original Looff Carousel anchored the pier's amusements from 1916 to 1939. Right: The Looff Hippodrome is listed on the National Register of Historic Places.

The Hippodrome as an Arts Center

For the entirety of its existence, the Looff Hippodrome has housed some very special, very distinct art—namely those beautiful, hand-carved wooden horses. But throughout the years the building has also hosted some very significant arts events.

In the spring of 1955, from May 18 through 27, artist Craig Kauffman, poet Ben Bartosch and his wife Betty, and Walter Hopps, co-curated a large independent show that was assembled and presented for the public to enjoy for free. The show was called "Action" and was the first in the Los Angeles area to feature the latest generation of West Coast Abstract Expressionist paintings. The entire carousel was wrapped in canvas tarps, covering the horses completely, and paintings were hung around the full exterior of the ride so that visitors could view them as they walked around the circular display. On occasion, the carousel was turned on, causing the display to slowly rotate. The visual show was accompanied by recorded jazz, plus a special version of John Cage's "Imaginary Landscape No. 4," which utilized transistor radios, each set at a different frequency to create a chaotic environment. Hopps, who was in the army at the time and co-curated remotely until the show opened, had a friend who lived in one of the apartments above the carousel and was able to secure the facility for relatively low rent. The show featured San Francisco-based artists including Jay DeFeo, Roy DeForest, Sonia Gechtoff, Hassel Smith, and Julius Wasserstein, and Los Angeles-based artists Gilbert Henderson, Craig Kauffman, and Paul Sarkisian. "Action" was well attended by the general pier-visiting public as well as by notables from the Beat movement including Allen Ginsberg and Jack Kerouac.

Folk music took over the Hippodrome in October 2013 and September 2014 as part of a music festival called "Way Over Yonder." While the larger part of the overall event took place on the parking deck outside of the building and featured artists such as Jackson Browne, the Hippodrome hosted smaller-sized and often acoustic acts including Frank Fairfield and Linda Perhacs, turning the facility into a casual and uniquely interesting music venue.

Live theater came next, in two different forms. In the spring months of 2017 and 2018 an intimate, two-person play called *An Illegal Start* used the carousel itself as the stage. Directed by Tony Award-winning actor Paul Sand, the play told the moving story of friendship between two people of completely different backgrounds and life paths, with scene breaks and time passage aided by the rotation of the carousel horses. In August 2018, a different theatrical experience produced by Cartel Arts Collaborative LA and called *The Friendship Show*, utilized the entirety of the space around the carousel with a series of short one-act presentations which the audience traversed the building to enjoy.

mysterious woman who frequented the building. In the early 1960s, an unknown woman, whose identity was concealed by an overcoat, sunglasses, and dark wig, regularly visited the carousel. The woman never rode the horses, just watched them circle around. Jockey, whose sentences were usually limited to only a word or two, approached her one day. While nobody is certain of their exact conversation, the woman uncovered her face and smiled, revealing her true identity. She was Marilyn Monroe.

On July 16, 1976, Thom O'Rourke and Mary Anne Hatala arranged to have their wedding ceremony performed on the carousel, exchanging vows while it was operating. It was a second marriage for both of the betrothed, and the groom wished to surprise his bride and her seven-year-old daughter with the special marriage site. It was the first recorded wedding at this historic site, and many more couples have since used the unique venue for their nuptials.

In 1977, the City of Santa Monica bought the carousel and the Hippodrome from the Gordon family for one hundred thousand dollars. The building and the horses had seen so much wear and tear throughout the years that the city ordered a full restoration. In 1980, they hired the sister/brother team Tracy and Steve Cameron to restore the horses to their once beautiful condition, while the building was stripped of its yellow stucco and red trim and refinished with the original colors of tan with blue trim. The rocking chairs surrounding the horses were replaced with a fenced and gated entrance that helped to prevent people from attempting to jump on to the merry-go-round as it was operating. The process took several months, and in June 1981, the newly finished horses were once again made available to the public. Carousel enthusiast Barbara Williams, the instigating force behind the restoration, assumed management of the carousel's operations in 1983 and continued with her labor of love for several years.

Among the last of its kind, the Hippodrome was adopted into the National Register of Historic Places on February 17, 1987. A bronze plaque denoting its landmark status is mounted on the north wall.

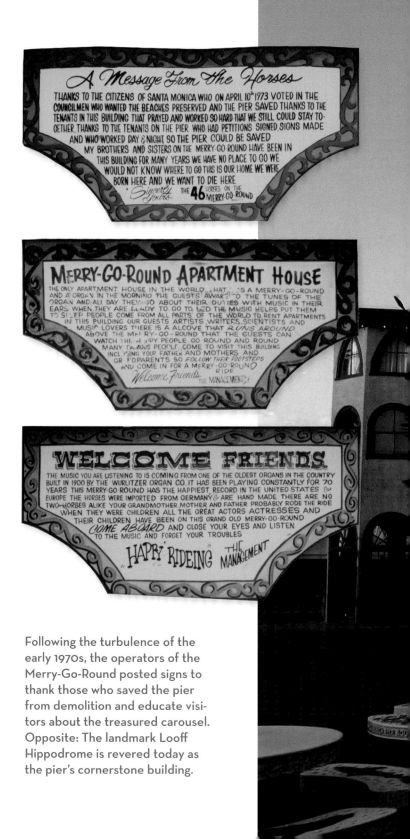

Following the turbulence of the early 1970s, the operators of the Merry-Go-Round posted signs to thank those who saved the pier from demolition and educate visitors about the treasured carousel. Opposite: The landmark Looff Hippodrome is revered today as the pier's cornerstone building.

Life Above the Horses

"The music, color, and laughter it generates provided many of us a refuge from the storms, both personal and political, of the late sixties and early seventies."
—Legendary folk singer Joan Baez, 2008

Some living spaces have inherent character. Some develop character through the people that have inhabited them. A very distinguished few are fortunate enough to have been touched by both. This is particularly true of the apartments above the carousel.

When the Looff family built the Looff Pleasure Pier in 1916, the first building erected was the Hippodrome. To be present during the construction, the Looffs took up residence in the newly built rooms on the building's second floor. While they old stayed through the construction period, they were the building's first inhabitants.

George Reid, one of the Looffs' managers for the construction project, also took advantage of the convenient living quarters so close to his work. He and his wife Winifred actually stayed there for several years, ample time to give birth to three children—George Jr., Winifred, and Catherine—inside their cozy apartment above the parading horses.

Since then, many people have called these unique living spaces home. As part of the magic that surrounds it, rumors have swirled about famous residents—no, W.C. Fields, Marilyn Monroe, Bob Dylan, Joan Baez, and Herb Alpert didn't live there, despite the legends. Nevertheless, those residents who actually lived above the horses were an interesting bunch. Artists, writers, poets, scientists, or just plain oddballs, the honored list is as wide ranging as is the description of those who have ever visited the pier.

In the 1920s, legendary stage and screen actor W.C. Fields was frequently seen ascending the outdoor steps that led to the upstairs apartments. A lifelong East Coast city dweller, the vaudevillian ventured from New York to Hollywood in 1925 to try his hand in the silent film business, making three movies with Paramount before returning to New York. Joining him on this venture was his good friend and on-stage stooge, William "Shorty"

Blanche. While the Hippodrome apartments were likely well below the standards that Mr. Fields was accustomed to, they suited Mr. Blanche just fine. He struck up residence above the carousel for several years, and his famous friend naturally stopped in for the occasional visit.

In 1944, Eric Jones accepted a job from Walter Newcomb to paint and maintain the carousel horses; the job came with an apartment upstairs. His wife and four daughters, Mona, Elaine, Barbara, and Essie, came with him. A gifted painter, Jones expanded his contribution by applying his talents to the crown-like canopy above the horses, whereupon he painted the postcard-like scenes that still decorate the structure today.

Iris Tree, an English poet and the daughter of actor Sir Herbert Beerbohm Tree, was one of the more notable occupants in the early 1950s. It is said that Ms. Tree had a natural beauty that drew the attention of several artists during her youth.

Writer/actor Tom Runyon moved into the apartment originally occupied by the Looffs in the late 1950s and, in 1961, he and his wife Barbara welcomed their first child, Allesandra. The trio remained in the Hippodrome apartment until 1964, then moved to Malibu where they opened a restaurant called The Old Place—still a Los Angeles-area favorite today.

In 1964, avant-garde filmmaker Bruce Conner rented out that same apartment in order to make a film with his friend, choreographer Toni Basil. Two years later they completed the project, a short film called *Breakaway*, which features Ms. Basil dancing to the song *Northern Soul* while she also sings on the soundtrack. Many people in the music and film industries consider this to be among the first and most influential music videos ever created.

Paul Sand, comic actor and playwright, lived in the southeast corner for a year in the late 1950s, trying

desperately to sleep in on weekend mornings while the Wurlitzer organ piped its merry, yet very loud, tunes. He left in 1959 for France where he would study in the more peaceful environment offered by mentor Marcel Marceau.

Edward Deland, a mathematician and scientist with the Rand Corporation, a United States government think-tank, moved into one of the apartments with his wife, Claire, in the mid-1950s. In the early 1960s the cou-

Longtime Hippodrome resident Tom Runyon enjoyed his living space above the carousel for more than a decade.

ple divorced, but Edward remained in the apartment until 1974—making him the longest-term resident of any Hippodrome apartment.

Writer William Saroyan never officially lived in the Carousel, but he rented one of its rooms as a work studio with friend and fellow writer Jimmy Henderson. While nothing substantial ever materialized from their writing partnership, it was Henderson's friendship with a future resident that would lend great impact to legend of the living spaces above the horses—Colleen Creedon.

A prominent Santa Monica activist, Ms. Creedon enjoyed two stints as a resident here: one from 1957 to

Folk music legend Joan Baez regularly enjoyed "crashing" at her friend Colleen Creedon's apartment in the 1960s and early 1970s.

powered by the sun, wind, and waves of its very environment. Beyond her activism, she was a vivacious member of the pier's everyday life. She is often remembered and referred to fondly as the "Lady above the Carousel," although her grandchildren gave her favorite label to her. They referred to her then, and still do today, as "Merry-go-round Granny."

In March 1974, the magical days of life above the horses came to an end. On March 4, arsonists set fire to the carousel building just below Creedon's apartment. Creedon actually saw the two young men set the fire and placed the 9-1-1 call to the fire department. Her husband bravely attempted to douse the flames with a fire extinguisher, but the fire spread too quickly. Thurber, the family dog, was trapped inside. Firemen arrived to battle the fire and managed to pull Thurber out through a window. They successfully put the fire out, but the damage to the building was already extensive. Within days, city officials ordered that the carousel apartments be vacated. The apartments above the horses became but a memory.

Some time later, the idea of a possible conspiracy entered Creedon's mind. While visiting with friends, she found out that the homes of two other female activists were targets of arson during the same week that she lost her cherished apartment. While she'll never know if she was a victim of political spite, she will always wonder…

In the 1980s, after the carousel's restoration, the rooms above the horses were reinhabited, but not as apartments. Today, the music that surrounds the circling horses drowns out the clicking of keyboards and the ringing of telephones from what are now the offices of the City of Santa Monica's Environmental Programs Department and the managers of the pier, the Santa Monica Pier Restoration Corporation.

1959, and one from 1966 to 1974. She utilized her unique living quarters to host fundraising parties to support the plights of Cesar Chavez and Daniel Ellsberg. Regular attendees of her parties included a handful of celebrities that were her friends. It was not uncommon to see Herb Alpert or Joan Baez climb the stairs to pay her a visit—presumably the root of the rumors much like the aforementioned W.C. Fields. She also organized the pier's celebration of Sun Day, a nationwide environmental event intended to raise awareness of the viability of solar energy. In fact, she even designed plans for a completely self-sufficient pier,

Bowling & Billiards

In 1917, Charles Looff completed the second structure on his pier, the Bowling & Billiards Building—home to Santa Monica Bowling Alleys. The venue featured eight bowling lanes, one Brunswick billiard table, and seven Brunswick pocket-billiards tables. Looff's goal was to maintain the most up-to-date amenities available, so he went to great efforts to obtain and install automatic pin-setting devices, a rarity at the time.

Santa Monica Bowling Alleys opened to the public on Wednesday, January 16, 1917. Mayor Samuel Berkley rolled the first ball, and then struck up a highly touted match against Police Chief Ferguson. The mayor should have stopped with the honor of rolling the first ball, for Ferguson out-bowled Berkley two games out of three. The police chief's prize for winning Santa Monica Bowling Alleys' first match was a silver-plated bowling pin. The consolation prize awarded the mayor was a bottle of ketchup. The night's activities proceeded with another highly anticipated match—the Los Angeles All-Stars versus the Santa Monica Home Guards. The Home Guards beat Santa Monica by winning two out of three games. Former local baseball star "Dad" Meek rolled the night's high score, an eyebrow-raising 225.

The bowling alley continued drawing crowds to league tournaments for several years. In the spring of 1924, Martin "Pop" Kern, three-time United States bowling champion, assumed management of the alleys, renaming the establishment Kern's Alleys. Pop, a national icon in the sport, proved to be an excellent manager and teacher who remained on the pier until his death in 1926. By the early 1930s, the pier's bowling alleys were just a memory.

Pool tables and bowling lanes filled the space within the appropriately named Looff Bowling & Billiards Building from 1917 well into the 1920s.

Al's Kitchen

Al's Kitchen, a small indoor/outdoor café, was known perhaps less for its food than for its patrons and the people who worked there. The restaurant, originally owned by and named after Al Bond, saw its brightest days under the waitress to whom he bequeathed it when he retired—an Englishwoman named Joan Crowne. It became a haven for local activists and artists, including politician Tom Hayden and actress Jane Fonda. Kitchen and waitstaff over the years included Julie Stone, one of today's more successful restaurateurs; Claude Bessy, the founder of the punk rock magazine *Slash*; Pat Lennon of the popular rock band Venice; celebrated Los Angeles poet FrancEyE; and Larry Barber, associate minister of the Founder's Church. It took a special person to manage a crew of this magnitude and talent, and Joan Crowne found that in Jack Sikking, former manager of some of Hollywood's most popular clubs. Legend has it that Sikking, fed up with Hollywood, walked out of his job one day and headed for the beach. He found himself walking along the deck of the pier when all of a sudden he felt as if he were home. Contemplating his life over a cup of coffee at the counter of Al's, he inquired about a job. Sikking was something of a visionary, and his interests extended far beyond the limitations of a small café. Within a short time, he had his hand in everything involved with the pier, and is generally credited as being the mastermind behind the efforts to save the pier from demolition in 1973.

O.J. Bennett's Seafood Grotto

In April of 1931, O.J. Bennett opened his Seafood Grotto on the Municipal Pier's north side. While it wasn't the first restaurant on the northern section of the pier's first "T," it became the most steadfast. The Grotto's original claim to fame was as an "open-air casino" where bridge parties were held over the waves under a colorful canopy. The north side "T" offered unobstructed, magnificent views of the ocean, the coast, and the Santa Monica Mountains. Bennett's seafood dishes were said to rival those of the great seafood restaurants in San Francisco, Baltimore, and New Orleans. Duncan Hines, the famous restaurant reviewer, visited the Grotto and enjoyed Bennett's broiled barracuda so much that he gave the restaurant a substantial review, referring to it in the *Saturday Evening Post* as "A place I want you to try."

O.J. BENNETT'S
SEA FOOD GROTTO

"CALIFORNIA'S MOST UNIQUE"

Specializing in

Sea Food
Cocktails

Clam Chowder

Fish Dinners

Santa Monica
Pier

Free Parking
To Our Patrons

Telephone
Santa Monica
28888

For more than thirty years, O.J. Bennett's Seafood Grotto occupied one of only two northside spaces on the pier. Opposite: A staged photo shoot outside of Al's Kitchen.

The Boathouse

In 1966, Paul and Sude Blank bought the Seafood Grotto from O.J. Bennett. Paul Blank was a well-known local artist who had previously owned an eclectic local bar called the Night Light. He changed the Grotto's name to The Boathouse and refinished the exterior with rustic looking burnt-wood siding. For financial assistance, the Blanks invited Sude's father, Benjamin DeSimone, to become their partner. DeSimone, a Boston-bred metallurgic engineer who worked as a consultant for the Atomic Energy Commission, assumed full ownership shortly afterward. Described by the *Evening Outlook* as a "colorful and gregarious man," DeSimone became well known in Santa Monica for his generosity. He would often purchase lunch or dinner for any uniformed law enforcement personnel he encountered, whether in his restaurant or in any other in which he happened to be dining.

The Boathouse, while known primarily as a seafood-and-steak house, also enjoyed a healthy reputation for its after-dinner live music. While much of the pier struggled to survive after the 1983 storms, The Boathouse secured itself as a primary destination and anchored the pier financially during its toughest stretch. DeSimone passed away in 1989, leaving the property in trust to his grandchildren. His younger daughter Patty, mother to the grandchildren, oversaw operations until her eldest daughter Naia was old enough to take over in 1996. The restaurant was expanded to include outdoor patios on both the pier and the beach level and its exterior was changed from deep brown to nautical gray. In the late 1990s and early 2000s, Sunday afternoon salsa dancing lessons were offered on the restaurant's beach level patio, becoming one of the most popular weekend afternoon destinations in Santa Monica.

Top, Left: Boathouse restaurant owner Ben DeSimone, 1980s. Top, Right: The two-story Boathouse restaurant was accessible from atop the pier and on the beach level. Bottom: Boathouse menu cover, 1990s.

The End Of Route 66?

What a romantic notion—the thought of driving iconic Route 66 all the way from Chicago to Santa Monica and taking in the sights and flavors of small town America from Navy Pier to Santa Monica Pier. Every year countless groups of people come parading down the pier ramp in their cars, their motorcycles, even on their bicycles, and celebrate the end of their journey across the country's storied 'Mother Road."

If only it were true.

While the Santa Monica Pier has often been labeled as the final destination of "Main Street of America," it just isn't so. There is a plaque in Palisades Park at the end of Santa Monica Boulevard, but that's not really the end either. According to the official record, US Route 66 ends at the corner of Olympic Boulevard and Lincoln Boulevard. But, after traveling 2,448 miles across the hot desert of the southwestern United States, who wouldn't want to end the journey with a drive under the landmark blue sign onto the cool world-famous pier.

Sinbad's

Besides the Hippodrome and the La Monica Ballroom, the most recognizable building on the pier was perhaps the brilliant red two-story structure known as Sinbad's. Originally built as the Looff Banquet Hall, the building was first located immediately adjacent to the west side of the Bowling & Billiards Building. In the mid-1920s, it was moved closer to the La Monica Ballroom, where it housed Hoyt's Chesapeake Café. After Hoyt's closed in 1955, the Newcombs' younger daughter Bette and her husband Dick Daily moved in, covered the entire structure in its famous red paint, and opened the pier's first up-scale restaurant. A comfortable, spacious restaurant with a fine view of the ocean, Sinbad's offered fare ranging from the standard seafood to beef stroganoff. It was well known for its lively bar atmosphere as well. Jay Fiondella, better known today for his eponymous legendary restaurant "Chez Jay," got his start in the hospitality business as a bartender at Sinbad's. The Dailys eventually separated and divorced, but Bette maintained the family business with her new husband, Dick Westbrook, until the mid-1970s.

The brilliant red Sinbad's restaurant building was the pier's defining structure prior to today's Pacific Park Ferris wheel.

The La Monica Ballroom

While the carousel building is by far the oldest, most established building on the pier, the La Monica Ballroom survives in memories and photographs as the most enigmatic. More than just a ballroom, the structure more closely resembled an enormous palace hovering over the sea. Its heyday was during the pier's most difficult years—an era of insecurity, uncertainty and, at times, despair. Its mere existence brought an occasional ray of hope, whether as a ballroom or as any of its other incarnations.

Hired to design the La Monica Ballroom, architect T.H. Eslick certainly knew how to make an impression. Built upon a footprint of more than forty thousand square feet and advertised as the largest ballroom in the world, the La Monica looked completely unique in its setting. Twelve minarets extending from each corner, combined with its curved facades and roof, lent a Spanish-style appearance, and the stucco exterior was designed to give the building the appearance of ancient stone. To decorate the interior, Eslick hired a group of Russian artists to create a submarine garden where dancers could revel in the illusion of dancing at the bottom of the ocean. Upholstered chairs and sofas provided exquisite comfort for the ballroom's guests, and extraordinary bell-shaped chandeliers floated above the ballroom floor, providing the only visible source of light—although it was obvious that other, hidden light sources were added to provide the ballroom's illumination. The lighting system was so extensive that the ballroom needed its own power facility, complete with three 120-horsepower engines that powered two generators.

Careful thought was given to each detail, all the way down to the management of the dance tickets and the location of the refreshment booths. The special "spring floor," which Eslick had designed himself to provide the most comfortable surface for dancing, received a lot of pre-opening buzz. Thirty-five thousand strips of hard maple were used to pattern the exquisite 15,000-square-foot floor.

It was no surprise that the ballroom drew as many as fifty thousand people to its premises on opening night. It was perhaps the most advertised affair Santa Monica had seen to date. Don Clark's Orchestra, among the most popular acts in the Los Angeles area at the time, was the night's featured performing artist. Dance tickets sold out right away, and the entire ballroom was limited to standing-room only throughout the gala event. Even with the flow of those attending just to have a look inside and then leave, the building was filled to capacity all night.

Ballroom attendance continued to thrive well after the dramatic opening night. Roy Randolph, a well-known local dance instructor, became a house fixture, teaching students of all ages and actively participating in the ballroom's special programs for Halloween, Christmas, and New Year's Eve. Don Clark's Orchestra played regularly, welcoming in guest artists like tuba player Carl Angeloty and band director Paul Whiteman. Film stars such as Bryant Washburn and Creighton Hale made guest appearances on a regular basis as well. The big dance craze at the time was the "Charleston," a provocative number originally developed to accompany the song of the same

name, and the La Monica capitalized on its popularity by hosting regular Charleston contests.

The great ballroom seemed invincible at the time, its popularity redefining the entire Santa Monica Pier. The ethereal vision of it floating above the ocean was perhaps even a bit symbolic. The humbling reality of nature voiced

The La Monica Ballroom was often described as a palace floating over the sea.

its authority, however, in the winter of 1926. On February 1, a storm devastated the California coast, completely destroying a small pier built at Santa Ynez Canyon and tearing loose pilings from the Municipal Pier. A boat landing that had been attached to the Municipal Pier broke loose and proceeded to rip loose piles beneath the La Monica Ballroom. The damage to the substructure caused the La Monica floor to sag and the entire structure to sway.

Repair of the pier and ballroom began almost immediately. The Santa Monica Amusement Company,

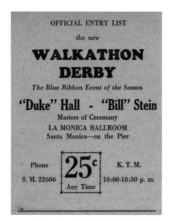

owners of the pleasure pier and the ballroom, hired Arthur Looff as a consulting engineer. Looff, happy to revisit his family's former enterprise, eagerly devised a method in which the new piles could be driven through the floor of the ballroom by means of hydraulic jettying. The process saved an enormous amount of time and money since the construction inflicted little damage to the rest of the structure. By early March, the work was complete and the ballroom was completely redecorated. The spring floor, completely destroyed by the storm, had been replaced by a new hardwood floor, touted to be even better than its predecessor.

On March 25, 1926, the La Monica Ballroom held its grand reopening celebration. Advertisements adorned the local newspapers much like they had during the original opening. Hollywood celebrities, including Sally Rand, were scheduled to appear, and Don Clark was once again tabbed to play the opening. The doors opened to a crowd estimated to be between five thousand and ten thousand, and the ballroom's popularity picked up right where it had left off. Dance contests, at this time featuring the waltz or the "foxtrot," were a regular draw. On Friday nights, contests for a new dance called the "Straight Collegiate" became very popular.

In August 1929, the City of Santa Monica hosted the National Women's Air Derby, an airplane race from Santa Monica to Cleveland, Ohio, which featured the world's top female pilots. On August 17, the night before the great competition, the La Monica Ballroom hosted

Left: Entry card for a Walkathon Derby held inside the ballroom in the early 1930s. Center: A meeting inside the La Monica Ballroom. Right: 1920s dance tickets for ballroom attendees. Opposite: Patrons line up at the bar inside the ballroom.

the Santa Monica Aviation Ball in honor of the acclaimed flying women. Competitors in the race and attendees at the ball included Florence Lowe "Pancho" Barnes, Ruth Elder, and the most famous female pilot in history, Amelia Earhart. The race ended in Cleveland nine days later with Earhart finishing third place behind Louise Thaden and Gladys O'Donnell.

In the summer of 1932, the La Monica offered relief for people who were out of work by hosting endurance contests. Originally introduced as "Walkathons," the events evolved into competitive dance endurance contests known as "Dance Marathons," a phenomenon that had become quite popular throughout the nation. The spaciousness and reputation as an entertainment venue made the La Monica an ideal locale for these entertaining, yet grueling, contests. Couples would compete for cash prizes ranging from one hundred to one thousand dollars by dancing nonstop for hours at a time, taking breaks only to eat and get a little bit of rest. The ballroom floor easily reached its five-thousand-person capacity at the onset of these marathons, and the contests regularly exceeded five hundred hours before a winner was determined. The

entertainment element was vital to the events; quarrels were staged and some competing couples were even married at the event. Brilliantly portrayed in the book and film *They Shoot Horses, Don't They?*, the contests were ultimately a very disturbing form of self-torture and unfulfilled hope for its participants. By the end of that summer, the city council deemed that the endurance contests were too brutal, and passed an ordinance outlawing any contest that would force participation for more than twenty-four hours.

In 1934, the City of Santa Monica was in need of a venue that could host large conventions, and entered into a lease agreement for the ballroom. The city's plan was to use it to the fullest of its capacity. Not only would it be the host venue for large conventions, but the weekly civic dances would be held there as well. Offices were also allocated for the Santa Monica Lifeguards and the Harbor Department, and the remaining spaces were leased to individual operators for a restaurant and other concessions.

Remodeling of the ballroom began the following

December. Lumber salvaged from movie studios was used in order to help keep expenses under control. Construction began with the lifeguard headquarters, located on the northeast corner of the massive structure. A special watchtower was created in the minaret above the lifeguard offices and the notion to install an aquarium inside the quarters was conceived.

James G. Frances originated the concept of displaying fish on the pier, and the plan quickly gained the support of many Santa Monicans, including television star Leo Carillo and comic strip writer E.C. Segar, the creator of "Popeye." Segar went so far as to share a letter of support to the *Santa Monica Evening Outlook* from the famous animated sailor:

"Dear Mr. Frances;
Tha's what I think too. Santa Monica should oughter have a aquarium. Folks loves to watch little fishes flittin about. It sorta

makes 'em relax an' feel kind of susperior. Gazin' at sculpin or barrycudales or even sourdings makes people realize what wonderful things hooman beings really are. So if a aquarium will make folks feel importink, then I sez, less have us a aquarium right here in good ol' Santa Monica. They's hunerds of reasings why we should have a aquarium an' ya kin put me down as bein in favor of it if ya'll promiss ya won't ast for no blasted donations. A' course if ya'll put in a bait tank for anchovies I might kick in with a donate.

Best fishes to you, I am:
Yers truly
Popeye"

The original suggestion for the location of the aquarium was on the newly constructed lower deck on the Municipal Pier, but the logical location of the display was inside the ballroom, under the supervision of the lifeguards. A four-thousand-pound tank and two smaller tanks were installed next to the headquarters in the recreation hall of the ballroom.

The city moved its traditional weekly civic dances into the ballroom while the construction proceeded, and held a New Year's Eve dance on December 31, 1934. Remodeling was complete in the summer of 1935, and on July 18, the La Monica Ballroom held yet another grand reopening as the La Monica Convention Auditorium and Recreation Hall. The aquarium opened as well, drawing large crowds every day. Charlie Chaplin and Paulette Goddard were known to be regular visitors, enjoying the display of garibaldi, small leopard sharks, and other fish found locally in the bay. In the late 1930s, "Oscar the Penguin," who had gained local fame on the Ocean Park Pier and was in need of a new place to stay after his home had been damaged by a storm, enjoyed a brief stay at the Santa Monica Pier Aquarium. He immediately made a nuisance of himself by eating all of the fish. Special arrangements were made for Oscar to be walked to the end of the pier and fed at Frank Volk's bait shop.

In May 1938, the ballroom was losing profitability and underwent another conversion, opening as the "Rollaway Roller Rink"—quite a distinct change from its previous uses within the community. As it turned out, the floor was quite suitable for skating.

In the latter part of 1938, Santa Monica was in the process of building a new city hall building, and the timing of the construction was such that the existing city hall building had to be vacated. Offices were subsequently relocated to various locations throughout the city and the La Monica was chosen as the new, temporary location for the police department and jail. During this period, the building that was once hailed as the largest, greatest ballroom in the world housed the city's lifeguards, police and prisoners in close quarters with fun-seeking roller skaters.

The temporary jail had quite a life of its own, despite its brevity. Twice there were reported jailbreaks, incidents that had not occurred in Santa Monica for many years. The first attempt was a futile endeavor by a seventeen-year-old boy confined in the jail's juvenile cell, charged with being a runaway. The boy tied blankets together, fixed one end to a water pipe, and threw the other end out the window. He began to climb through the window, only to discover that he was too big to fit through. A lifeguard passed by a short while later, saw the boy's dangling legs outside the window, and contacted the police inside.

The second jailbreak was considerably more successful, though not completely. A twenty-nine-year-old man who had been booked for robbery escaped early in the morning, by prying the steel grill from his cell's window, climbing outside, and leaving the pier by foot. His absence was discovered at seven a.m. and a radio alert was sent out immediately. Two police officers happened to see the escaped prisoner hitchhiking at the corner of Wilshire and San Vicente just as the alert came over the radio, picked him up, and immediately brought him back to the pier jail. Upon questioning the man, police discovered the night watchman had given him a can of snuff from which he used a sharp piece of steel to loosen the jail window's grill, thereby enabling his escape.

Left: Albert Otis Bryan, a twenty-nine-year-old man arrested for robbery, explains to a police detective exactly how he escaped the city jail, which was temporarily located inside the ballroom. Center: Voucher for the Spade Cooley show inside the ballroom, late 1940s. Right: Early 1960s souvenir sticker from the ballroom's days as a roller skating rink.

Neither the roller rink nor the jail remained in the ballroom for long. By the end of 1939, the rink had closed and the police department moved into its new city hall location on Main Street. Some of the rooms on the perimeter of the ballroom were made available for lease as apartments. In 1943, the center of the ballroom was even used for badminton competitions, but it wasn't until the late 1940s that new life truly began to be infused into the great building.

Western Swing music swept the nation throughout the 1940s. It first achieved popularity just prior to World War II and again after the war. The ballroom welcomed the new sound, reopening as an entertainment venue. The name La Monica had not been used since before the facility's convention center days. For a brief time, the renewed venue was dubbed the Western Palisades Ballroom and then the Santa Monica Ballroom. Regardless of the name, Western Swing was the new game, and it played well.

Spade Cooley, famous for the 1945 hit "Shame on You," was the self-proclaimed "King of Western Swing," and in the 1940s, he established a home in the ballroom. His regular appearances there became so popular that, on August 5, 1948, TV-station KTLA made Cooley the first variety act to be performed live on television. His show,

called the "Hoffman Hayride," immediately became one of the most popular weekly television shows on the air. Called the "Hoffman Hayride" to call attention to the show's sponsor, a TV-set manufacturer, the production focused entirely on Cooley and his band. The name was eventually changed to "The Spade Cooley Show." Stan Chambers, longtime news anchor and familiar face on local television, got his start doing commercial spots for Cooley's show during its heyday.

Dick Lane, also of KTLA, did live car commercial pitches direct from Cooley's show and created a bit of his own television notoriety. During one of his broadcasts, Lane got frustrated with the crowd talking over him, so he pounded his fist upon the advertised car's fender. This quieted the crowd and drew the attention that he desired, so Lane adopted the routine as part of his act until one night he hit the fender so hard that it fell off the car, resulting in what has since been regarded as a classic comic moment in live television history.

"The Spade Cooley Show" continued with great success in the Santa Monica Ballroom until March 1954, when the show was relocated to the KTLA studios. By 1956, increasing competition and a lack of fresh ideas for the show resulted in sagging ratings. Cooley began to drink heavily and developed a surly attitude. In 1957, he was fired. In 1961, he was convicted of murdering his wife Ella Mae. He served eight years in prison and was released on good behavior. He made one more live appearance before passing away after a heart attack on November 23, 1969.

Automobiles once again became the featured attraction of the La Monica when the Hollywood Auto Museum occupied the Ballroom in 1955. Cars on display dated all the way back to an 1898 French-made DeDion Buttoon, and included Marlene Dietrich's sixteen-cylinder Cadillac (gas mileage: four miles per gallon), Rudolph Valentino's Lancia, and the Auto-Union Horch that Adolph Hitler gave to his lover, Eva Braun. Notable celebrities such as

Gary Cooper attended opening day of the show.

In 1961, the ballroom opened again as a roller rink, but the aging structure's roof had begun to sag and the walls showed signs of buckling; hopes for new success stemming from the popular roller derbies collapsed along with the building's integrity. In July 1962, the building was roped off and closed to the public. After lengthy evaluation, officials ordered the demolition of the great La Monica Ballroom, leaving behind a vast, empty lot.

Parking was available on the deck immediately in front of the entrance to the ballroom.

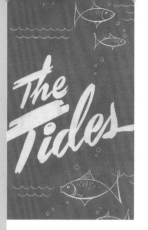

Santa Monica Seafood

In 1939, brothers Frank and Jack Deluca founded Santa Monica Seafood Company on the north side of the Municipal Pier selling fresh catches of fish such as halibut, sea bass, mackerel, and sardines. The Delucas' timing for opening on the pier was fortunate, for during World War II, Santa Monica harbor became a focal point for commercial fishing boats to unload their catches; Santa Monica Seafood subsequently became one of the primary distributors of seafood. Thousands of tons of fish, primarily mackerel, were unloaded onto the pier and trucked away by the Delucas regularly, so much so that in 1942, engineers considered the Municipal Pier deck to be too stressed by the loads. The Delucas fought to keep business flowing, and even offered to take responsibility should significant damage happen as a result of the heavy loads. Ultimately, they were forced to lighten their loads until the city could repair the deck and substructure so it could handle significant weight. While this put a damper on the Delucas' business during a crucial time of the war, Santa Monica Seafood survived on the pier throughout the next couple of decades, until it moved inland a few blocks.

Located on the north side of the pier, Santa Monica Seafood was the pier's primary fresh seafood retail operation until 1969.

The Galley and The Tides

As Santa Monica Yacht Harbor prepared to open its operations, businessmen carefully eyed the Santa Monica Pier for the obvious opportunities that would accompany it. Ralph Stephan was among those, and in 1934, he opened a small, nautically themed restaurant on the end of the amusement pier, just west of the La Monica Ballroom. He called his restaurant The Galley. Advertised as "A unique South Seas setting" with "twinkling lights and bobbing" and offering "shore dinner deluxe," The Galley was a natural for the pier, catering to the community of seagoing yachtsmen so anticipated by the opening of the new harbor. Stephan proudly boasted on his menu "Our own fishing boats bring in our fish and lobsters daily."

The Galley enjoyed a successful run on the pier until 1946, when Stephan was forced to move his restaurant off of the pier to make room for a yacht club—that never opened—and left the building vacant after The Galley's departure. Stephan moved his business to Main Street, where it still operates with the honor of being the oldest restaurant in Santa Monica.

Since the ballyhooed plans for the yacht club fell through, Santa Monica Seafood's Jack Deluca took advantage of the vacancy left by The Galley. After all, it was conveniently located directly opposite the Municipal Pier from his business, and supplying it with fresh caught seafood would be no problem. He opened it in May 1946, under the not-so-original name The New Galley, later changing the name to The Tides Café. Realizing that restaurant management was not really his forte, Deluca sold The Tides to his manager, Joe Guggenmos, in the 1950s. Guggenmos continued to operate it, using fish bought from the Delucas, for well over a decade. The café closed in the early 1970s.

Blue Streak Racer

The Blue Streak Racer was a racing-style coaster; it had two tracks running side-by-side with cars on each track running simultaneously, literally racing through the coaster's six loops and twenty-four dips. The Blue Streak reached an apex of sixty-five feet and ran its cars across a mile of track. Upon its opening, it was described as one of the most thrilling rides on the Santa Monica Bay.

The Whip and Aeroscope

When riding The Whip, two passengers would ride side-by-side in a small car around a course shaped like a racetrack. At each end of the track were turns that cars would take at such great speed that riders were forced together as they whipped around each curve. Passengers rode the giant Aeroscope in "flying boats" that swung at angles of nearly forty-five degrees, circling the central core at speeds up to forty-five miles an hour. Riders could not lift their bodies from the seats no matter how hard they tried, the physics of the swing keeping them secure in their boats.

The Whip, one of the pier's first thrill rides, 1917. Opposite: The pier's first roller coaster, the Blue Streak Racer, opened August 3, 1916. It ran two tracks side-by-side, giving riders the extra sensation of racing the car on the track next to them.

The Whirlwind Dipper

A former pilot from Canada, C.B. McConnely, commented that his experience riding the Whirlwind Dipper was comparable to that of flying in a stunt plane, giving him chills up and down his spine. That summed it up for adults, but it took a child to really capture the coaster's allure.

The *Evening Outlook* newspaper billed the Whirlwind Dipper as "The Greatest Ride Ever Built," but wanted to get an honest opinion from those who would be its most loyal riders—children. So they held an essay contest through the newspaper. The child who wrote the best letter describing the towering, twisting new coaster would receive a season pass. Young Ben McFee of Santa Monica won with the following letter:

"Hold tight all the way and don't stand up," shouted the man and then we were off. Before I could count ten we had passed through the spooky tunnel and were on our way to the top of the big dip. That was the minute that seemed like a year. I got cold and then hot, and I turned all colors of the rainbow before I reached the top of the big dip. Oh boy, here we go Yeh-h-h-h Boo-o-o! Gee what a dip, and here we come to another one, and another one, and another one and, gee-whiz, how many more are there? I've lost my breath. I wish they would stop this thing for a minute. Good night, aren't we nearly through yet? That last dip almost threw me out, and here we go down another one. Oh my! What a funny sensation that was. This thing goes too fast to suit me, and all I hope is that I reach the bottom alive. "Have your fares ready, please." What sound could be sweeter? For at last we have reached the bottom, and I am still alive, thank goodness. Just the same, the ride was great and the best ever. I surely did as the man commanded me, for I never held on so tight in all my life. As for "don't stand up," well it was all I could do to stay in my seat. Of all the excitement, speed and thrills, well all I have to say is that the Whirlwind Dipper is by far the best ride yet. Fellows, if you want to get the kick of your life, just try the new Whirlwind Dipper once, for it sure is some wicked ride.

With an endorsement like that, the *Evening Outlook* offered free rides on the coaster to all children who clipped out the ad and presented it for admission. What parent could say "no" to buying the paper?

The much more thrilling Whirlwind Dipper roller coaster replaced the Blue Streak Racer in the early 1920s.

Bumper Cars

In 1972, amusement entrepreneurs Maynard and Sheila Ostrow opened the bumper car ride near the amusement pier's west end. The electric cars, powered by an overhead grid, quickly became a favorite attraction on the pier. Perhaps even more notable than the ride was the classic, "antique" ticket booth. In truth, however, the old booth was even newer than the bumper cars themselves. The Ostrows commissioned employees of Al's Kitchen to build the booth. Jack Sikking, manager of Al's and a close friend of the Ostrows, suggested that the newly built ticket booth be distressed for vintage, "worn" look. He assumed the job of finishing it himself, and the results were so convincing that tourists and even museum curators began to inquire about the value of the "old antique."

Top: The pier's bumper cars were a "must" for visitors to enjoy in the latter decades of the twentieth century. Center and Bottom: The owners paid meticulous attention to the appearance of their ticket booth.

Pacific Park

When Pacific Park welcomed the public in May 1996, it was the first time that visitors were able to enjoy a permanent amusement park on the Santa Monica Pier in sixty-six years. Since the removal of the Whirlwind Dipper and other thrill rides in 1930, the only long-term installations were the merry-go-round (since 1916) and the bumper cars (1972 to 1995). Interspersed throughout the years were a number of temporary installations that included go-carts in the 1960s, a giant slide in the 1970s, and a traveling summertime carnival in the 1980s and early 1990s. Pacific Park harkened back to the early days of not only the Looff Pleasure Pier, but also the great amusement park piers in Venice and Ocean Park as well. From its opening day, the park has been committed to welcoming people without admission fees, and remains the only free amusement park in the Los Angeles area.

Pacific Park's new thrill rides included a roller coaster, a dragon swing, and a towering Ferris wheel named the Pacific Wheel. The Pacific Wheel quickly became the pier's new visual icon, featured on both local newscasts and on national broadcasts. In 1998, its power source was converted to solar energy, making it the first solar-powered Ferris wheel in the world. After twelve years on the pier, however, the wheel succumbed to the effects of the marine environment. In May 2008, Pacific Park sold the wheel to an Oklahoma developer through the Internet auction company eBay for $130,400, half of which the park donated to the Special Olympics of Southern California. A new wheel, identical in size and specifications, was installed. The new wheel boasts one outstanding new feature—a lighting system with 160,000 new energy-efficient solar-powered LED lights, capable of changing colors and patterns from one moment to the next. On May 28, 2008, the new Pacific Wheel was unveiled to the public, accompanied by the pier's first firework show since 1990. In 2016, the wheel received another enhancement, increasing the LED light quantity to 174,000 lights with higher resolution and faster "frames per second," allowing for the wheel to display highly detailed artwork, imagery, and messaging.

In April 2023, another ride, the highly popular Sea Dragon, was retired and replaced with a new, almost identical version, albeit with new enhancements. In a special ceremony to replace the old with the new, the original Sea Dragon was removed from the pier via helicopter.

Pacific Park has also become a favorite event venue for local organizations and celebrity-events alike, including its highly publicized use as a wedding reception venue for socialite/media personality Paris Hilton.

During the restoration and reimagination of the pier after the 1983 storms, the prevailing dream was to make the Santa Monica Pier more family friendly. The opening of Pacific Park in 1996 ushered in that new era, paving the way for the pier to become a premiere destination that millions of visitors enjoy every year.

The Best Fishing in the Bay

When John McCreery landed the first yellowtail a week before the pier opened in 1909, word spread quickly—the Santa Monica Pier was one of the finest fishing spots on the coast. Not a day passed that the Municipal Pier wasn't crowded with anglers waiting to hook a halibut, perch, corbina, or another finned prize. About the same time, an eighty-two-year-old man boasted that he fished at the pier twice a day, and would do so until the day he died. He did. Swarms of children regularly went to the pier after school to try their luck at landing some sort of sea creature. In July of 1910, a husband/wife team wrestled a thirty-five pound black sea bass onto the pier deck, the largest fish landed at the pier to that date.

Fishing gear ranged from primitive "jack poles" and "knuckle-busters" to the more elaborate rods 'n' reels—whatever could effectively haul a hooked critter up from its Pacific home was considered fair tackle. Small shops—stands, really—cropped up along the deck offering pole rentals and bait for sale, the first business enterprises on the pier.

Some members of the fishing community assumed territorial behavior. Arguments erupted over fishing spots. But when the Looff Pleasure Pier was built adjacent to the Municipal Pier in 1917, a big group of fishermen were infuriated. The deck of the new pier was laid directly over the best haven for croakers in the entire bay. Captain Al Green, superintendent of the Municipal Pier, quickly

Since the beginning, the pier's most loyal community has been those with fishing poles who, if asked, will declare that no matter what other amenities adorn the structure, it is first and foremost a fishing pier.

retracted a joking suggestion that the fishermen cut holes in the wooden deck and drop their lines through to the ocean (much like ice fishermen do on frozen winter lakes) for fear that some irate anglers would take him seriously and pose a hazard to pedestrians.

On June 23, 1922, W.H. Bakerbour landed a fish that shattered all previous records. The fish, a 450-pound black sea bass, took over an hour and every ounce of Bakerbour's strength to land. The pier experienced a run on these fish in the early 1920s, but fishermen on sport fishing boats caught them more often. Sometimes referred to as Sea Hippos, the fish could reach a length of eight feet, weigh over five hundred pounds, and could live to be over sixty years old.

For anglers who weren't satisfied with simple pier fishing, boating operations offered daily service from the pier's west end. In the summer of 1921, Captain Thornton J. Morris began the pier's first fishing excursion boat operations. T.J., as he was known, offered private charters aboard the sixty-foot cabin cruiser *Ursula* and the speedboat *Josie M* and within a couple of years he expanded the fleet, adding the sixty-foot *Ameco,* the *Palisades,* and *W.K.* Competition followed. By the mid-1920s, the pier offered sportfishing fare aboard boats such as Dick Hernage's *Scandia* and *Bright I,* Olaf Olsen's *Harold O.* and *Viking* and Scotty Lacade's *Kitty A.* For those less adventurous about taking a day trip, but still willing to brave deeper waters, a small fleet of fishing barges was anchored in the bay and fishermen took water taxis to reach them.

The greatest "heyday" of boating activity at the pier was the 1940s. While the Second World War had effectively pushed the bulk of the yachting community out of the harbor in favor of fishing boats, the change in purpose certainly did not change the amount of activity. Among the notables within the fishing community was June Scroggins, one of the few female certified fishing boat captains of the era and the only woman among the captains who claimed Santa Monica as their home port.

As it departed, the pier's boating operations shrunk to two sport fishing boats: Bill Pelton's *Indiana* and Karl Demmit's *Kiaora,* each of which continued to operate until the storms of 1983 effectively put an end to all of the pier's boating operations.

Anglers remain the most loyal visitors to the pier. Occasionally a run of bonito will swarm the pier, jolting it full of so much energy and life that it's easy to conjure the excitement of those days when the pier was the fishing capital of Santa Monica Bay. Perhaps that's the real reason fishermen come to the pier each day—any day might be *that* day.

Left: Fishermen Dick Hernage and Frank Vok pose with a giant Black Sea Bass, a common species caught at the pier in the early twentieth century. Center: The fishing boat *Bright I* was one of the most popular day trip boats in the mid-twentieth century. Right: June Scroggins built and captained her own fishing boat, primarily operating from the pier in the 1940s.

The Tragic Tale of the Morris Fleet

T.J. Morris, the man who started it all, was the pier's most unfortunate fisherman—tragedy struck him in threes. First, on the night of April 3, 1924, the *Ursula* broke free from her mooring and began to drift out to sea. Morris, determined to rescue his prized boat, caught up to her in a small skiff, climbed aboard, and attempted to start her gasoline engine. The engine backfired, ignited the *Ursula,* and nearly took his life. Morris was able to escape the floating inferno, drifting away aboard the same skiff he rowed out on. Fishermen on the Municipal Pier rescued him later. In 1926, the Morris flagship *Ameco* broke her mooring during a February storm. The boat drifted into the Municipal Pier, battered against the pilings hard enough to cause extensive damage to the pier, and ultimately was smashed to bits.

On April 8, 1926, Captain Morris again found himself chasing after one of his vessels. This time it was the *W.K.* that broke loose in a storm and found itself on a course bent on ramming into the pier. Morris and two crewmen, Leo Gregory and Paul Brooks, jumped aboard a small skiff and set forth to rescue the drifting ship. As the three men approached the *W.K.* a massive breaker overturned the skiff, casting all three men into the sea. Moments later they reached and righted the skiff, as a growing crowd on the pier watched. Captain Morris struggled to save his crewmen, so his son-in-law Jack Duggan quickly organized a rescue party. The team rowed toward the accident while lifeguards jumped into the ocean from the beach, carrying rescue cans to help the struggling sailors. All efforts were futile. The crew disappeared from sight. Leo Gregory was the first to be found as he lay dying underneath the Crystal Pier, about a half-mile south. The bodies of Paul Brooks and T.J. Morris were recovered a few days later.

The *W.K.* fared far better—she washed ashore several hundred yards away from the pier. The *W.K.* continued service in the Morris fleet under the stewardship of T.J.'s cousin Clifford Morris. The fleet expanded in 1929 to include new boats *I.K.I., Lois, Colleen, Morris Owl, Lark,* and a second *Ameco.*

On May 30, 1930, a Memorial Day excursion aboard the new *Ameco* went terribly awry. The fishing boat had been loaded beyond its passenger capacity and headed into rough seas near Santa Monica Canyon. A strong wind whipped showers of water across the boat, causing most of the passengers to assemble on its lee side to avoid the annoying spray. A huge swell caught and capsized the already listing boat, sending all of her passengers into the ocean. Another fishing boat, Dick Hernage's *Freedom*, was fortunately also in the area, and was able to pick up many of the castaway passengers. Since records on excursion boats were poorly kept at the time, nobody was certain how many people were aboard the *Ameco*. After a long search during which fifty-four people were rescued, it was determined that sixteen people had probably perished. The lack of clarity surrounding the incident combined with the overcrowding of passengers drew serious scrutiny from both the coast guard as well as city and county governments, and new regulations were quickly adopted to avoid such a horrible event from occurring again.

A full fishing boat in the water near the location of the short-lived "Morris Pier" extension of the Santa Monica Pier.

The End of the Pier (West End, That Is)

People seem to have a need to go as far as they can, to break the barriers established by Mother Nature. The west end of the pier fulfills that need, providing the power that people unconsciously seek. Home to the fishing community, fondly remembered by the boating community, and tempted by the fury of the sea, the end of the pier has had a colorful life of its own. It grew beyond being an "end." Rather, it is a way for visitors to connect more closely with the sea.

Beginning on opening day in 1909, ships from the United States naval fleet regularly anchored a short distance from the end of the pier. The first such ships were of the cruiser and battleship classes—the USS *Albany*, the USS *Maryland*, the USS *Arizona,* and several others stopped by Santa Monica for a little rest and relaxation. In later years, aircraft carriers such as the USS *Saratoga (CV-3)* and the USS *Lexington (CV-2)* visited, the huge ships silhouetted against the hori-

A rescue crew attempts to save the sinking water taxi, ironically named *Good News*, 1948. Opposite: Santa Monica Sport Fishing was always the center of activity at the pier's west end, where patrons could rent fishing poles, buy bait, and purchase fare for a fishing boat excursion.

previously existing Standard Oil gasoline facilities were moved to the lower deck for better access. Finally, three inches of asphalt were laid over the upper level decking. By 1937, the rest of the Municipal Pier and the Pleasure Pier were covered with asphalt as well.

The lower level cultivated a thriving life of its own. The lifeguards kept quarters on the far west side, around the corner from the Standard Oil station. In the 1960s, the Standard Oil station vacated the lower deck, and in 1965, the Oatman Rock Shop took over the space. Other businesses that occupied the lower deck were the Port Hole Café and the Below Deck Café.

Countless storms have unleashed their fury on the west end, boats have slammed into its pilings, and debris from less fortunate piers have battered it, yet through decades it stood its ground. Perhaps the most frightening event in its history had little to do with the ocean at all. In the summer of 1945, the twenty-eight-foot fishing boat *Nadine*, recently put into the water after an overhaul, filled up her fuel tank with 250 gallons of gasoline at the Standard Oil station. As her captain, Bert Taylor, turned on the boat's ignition, a spark ignited gasoline that had spilled onto the deck. The boat's fuel tank exploded, blowing the hatch of the boat two hundred feet straight up into the air as the rest of the boat became engulfed in flames. Taylor miraculously escaped with only minor burns. Quick action by the lifeguards, Santa Monica Fire Department and U.S. Coast Guard kept the fire from spreading onto the pier and igniting the Standard Oil station.

In 1948, a water taxi for the fishing barge *Trade Winds* was found slowly sinking about a half-mile off of the pier by a passing fishing boat, the *Linbrooke*. The taxi, ironically named *Good News*, was lost in thick fog and

zon stealing the breath away from hundreds of onlookers. Sailors came ashore and water taxis carried civilians who toured the ships.

When the long-anticipated Santa Monica Yacht Harbor became a reality, the west end drew even more attention. In 1934, the city extended and expanded it, adding a second level below the west and north sides of the pier, suspended approximately eight feet above the water. Offices for the harbormaster were constructed on the southwest corner of the upper level in 1934 and the

The lower fishing deck at the pier's west end; among its many attractions was the Port Hole Cafe, a coffee shop that remained open twenty-four hours a day.

taking on water when the *Linbrooke* happened upon her. Knee deep in water, the forty-three passengers of the *Good News* climbed to safety aboard the fishing boat. The *Linbrooke* then towed the waterlogged boat to the Municipal Pier. The boat all but sank completely below the west end, but Harbormaster Pat Lister and lifeguard Frank Donahue managed to hoist her to the dry dock for repairs.

Such commotions did not spoil matters for the fishing community. Everything else around the fishermen—the boating, the cafés, the stores—was fine as long as there was still space to drop a line in the water to reel in a mackerel. Only once in the last half of the twentieth century was that public fishing space in jeopardy. In 1965, the South Coast Corinthian Yacht Club, having tried for decades to secure a private clubhouse on the pier, sought to lease a significant amount of the lower deck, one of the most popular fishing spots on the entire west end. The city liked the idea of receiving rental income, but fisherwoman-turned-activist Diana Cherman organized a protest and, along with a school of fishermen, protested

to the council members. Cherman insisted that there was more at stake than money. The pier was for all people—"a public pier," she insisted, adding that money should never dictate who uses a public pier. The scrappy little bunch prevailed, and the fishing spot was saved.

Today's west end experience is considerably different than that of the pre-storm/restoration days, but the area is no less revered. Fishing activity still exists, and the community of anglers remains the most loyal to the pier as they are present day and night, rain or shine. In addition, the end of the pier has become a favorite spot for events including Saturday morning yoga and other fitness activity, silent disco events on weekend evenings, and a play called *"Save the Pier!"* which recounts the early-1970s community fight to save the pier from demolition. Street performers relish the area as a preferred performance place. It has also become a favorite location for press conferences and even the occasional wedding. Perhaps the most regular crowd (save for the fishing community) is the group of people who have discovered the west end bleachers as

being the perfect place to watch the sunset in hopes of witnessing the optical phenomenon known as the "green flash." Indeed, whether the day ends with the sun setting over Malibu in the summertime or over the Pacific Ocean in the wintertime, the end of the pier has become an ideal and coveted location for viewing the passing of daytime into twilight into night.

Wildlife, fun activities and camaraderie defined the pier's west end from the 1930s until 1983, when violent storms washed it all away. Opposite: Motorists and pedestrians alike enjoyed the ability to travel all the way to the end of the pier. While vehicles are no longer allowed, pedestrians are still able to walk the 1,600-foot-long pier to enjoy life above the ocean.

Harbor Patrol Caretakers of the Pier

As the completion of the breakwater and official opening of Santa Monica Yacht Harbor drew near, Santa Monica city officials recognized the need to create a department to oversee the new harbor's expected 230 mooring spaces, a vital new income source. In August 1934, the city created a new Harbor Administration under the supervision of City Commissioner H.C Sanborn and four Deputy Harbormasters E.G. Bailey, George Watkins (Captain of the Santa Monica Lifeguards), George T. Mills (Manager of Municipal Pier), and Owen Churchill (Chairman of the Harbor Board). Together these individuals made up what later became known as the Harbor Department and is known today as Harbor Patrol. Throughout its history the Harbor Department's primary purpose was oversight and maintenance of the breakwater, harbor moorings, and the pier's boat access. With the devastation of the storms of 1983, however, the department's duties changed significantly. Suddenly, there was no real harbor to maintain. Still, the department persevered, for while boats could no longer be moored in the harbor, there was still the very important need to maintain and secure the area around the remnants of the breakwater, which had become mostly a submerged reef, and to regularly inspect and maintain the piles. Additionally, the city needed an organization to act as round-the-clock "eyes and ears." The Harbor Department has since become known as Harbor Patrol, a division of the Santa Monica Police Department, with a specially skilled crew who fulfill the dual roles of underwater maintenance and on-the-pier activity supervision. Each member of this team is a certified lifeguard and skilled first responder, with skills that also translate into public relations as they are among the most visible of all of the pier's workforce.

Moby's Dock

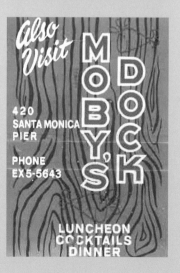

Also Visit
MOBY'S DOCK

420
SANTA MONICA
PIER

PHONE
EX5-5643

LUNCHEON
COCKTAILS
DINNER

Moving their operations into the vacant building that was formerly The Tides Café, the Westbrooks redecorated and opened a new restaurant named Moby's Dock. They decorated the restaurant with red-checked tablecloths and an appropriately nautical theme. The exterior of the building was decorated with paintings of cartoon-like whales and a large white whale tail sculpture that appeared as though the great Moby Dick himself had crashed into the restaurant looking for a bite to eat. In 1977, the Westbrooks sold the restaurant to Clarence Harmon. Harmon kept the name and Moby's Dock thrived until the storms of 1983 caused such damage to the restaurant, both structurally and to the overall business, that Harmon was unable to keep up with rent payments. In 1984, Harmon was evicted and Moby's Dock closed its doors for good.

While the Moby's Dock structure has long since vanished from the pier, its trademark white whale's tail has managed to surface in various locales around the pier. After the demolition of Moby's, Ben DeSimone acquired the sculpture and had it placed prominently at the front of The Boathouse. From there, the tail waved to millions of passersby until this second home found a fate similar to its first. As The Boathouse was being razed, the Pier Maintenance crew rescued the tail, and gave it a new home above their workshop. A true survivor, this resilient piece of décor has developed something of a kinship with the pier.

Moby's Dock was the pier's most popular restaurant in the 1970s and early 1980s, largely because of its amazing ocean view.

Doreena Adams and her family told fortunes on the pier for more than half a century.

The Boardwalk Over Time

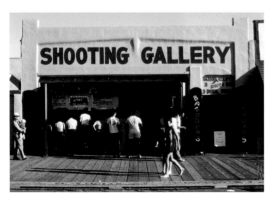

Some places are just plain unforgettable, not for any particular reason other than they defined a place in time. To the people who saved the pier in 1973, the row of shops and cafés between the Hippodrome and Moby's Dock did just that. They defined their beloved pier.

Occupying the old Bowling & Billiards Building was a series of such distinct businesses. Beryl's Art Novelties Studio occupied the east side, displaying in its front windows a variety of ceramic lamp bases, figurines, and masks. Next to it was the Fish 'n' Chips café, well known for its homemade potato chips, whose aroma wafted across the entire pier and became so famous that modern-day restaurant legend Bob Morris purchased the restaurant in 1978, just to be a part of what had become a great pier tradition. Seaview Seafood, an open-air fresh-fish market traditional to piers and wharfs everywhere, was just beyond it. Selling fish and shellfish caught from the boats that regularly serviced the pier, the Seaview was a destination spot for anyone with an appetite for good, fresh seafood.

Clara's, a fast food café, fed hungry visitors with hot dogs and ice cream, and next to it was a haven for souvenir shoppers—the Beachcomber gift shop. An assortment of booths stood a bit further west, housing carnival games such as the milk can toss and basketball shoot. Surrounded by the chaos of these games, somewhat like the eye of a hurricane, was the spiritual office of Doreena, the pier's longtime fortune teller. Operated by the Dewey Adams family, Doreena's moved onto the pier in 1943, when the City of Santa Monica passed an ordinance that stated that the only place in which fortune-telling was permitted was on the area's amusement piers. As popular with those who sought serious spiritual guidance as with those who just wanted to have a little fun, fortunes told by generations of Adamses were long a vital part of the pier's fabric.

Playland Arcade holds the distinction of being the longest family-run business ever operated on the pier. Owned by the George Gordon family since 1954, the "last arcade in Santa Monica" is now managed by the fourth generation of the family.

Beyond Sinbad's stood the ballroom (until it was torn down in 1963) and the Cocky Moon Snack Bar, a quirky little fast-food restaurant featuring a walk-up window with the menu hand-painted above in large, bold lettering.

Top to Bottom: The Looff Hippodrome, Beryl's Art Novelties, the Fish 'n' Chips café, and Shooting Gallery were all beloved staples on the pier. Opposite: A day at the pier in the 1970s and '80s was never complete without a visit to the walkup window at the Cocky Moon.

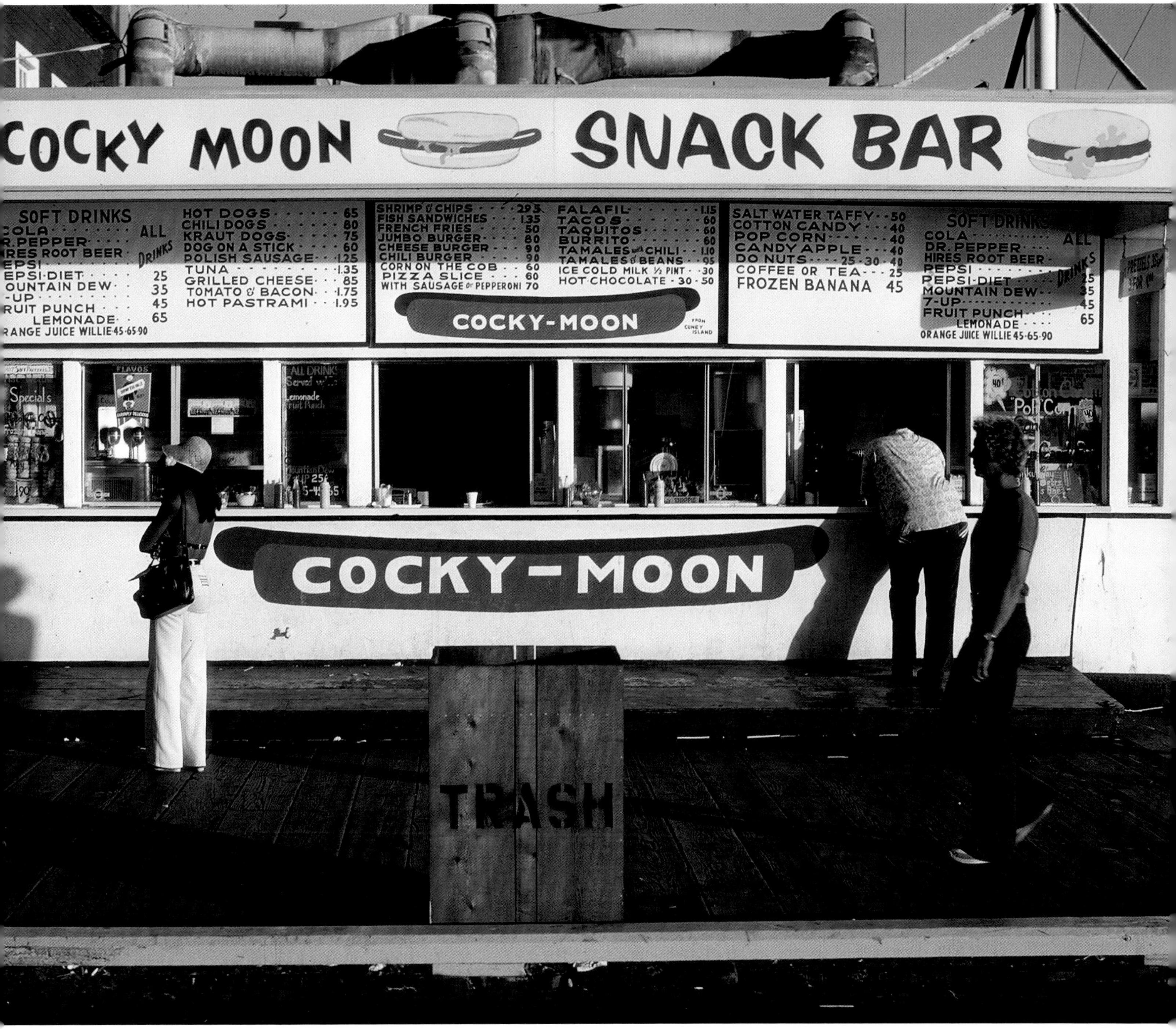
COCKY MOON
SNACK BAR
SOFT DRINKS
ALL DRINKS
25
35
45
65
LEMONADE
HOT DOGS 65
CHILI DOGS 80
KRAUT DOGS 75
DOG ON A STICK 60
POLISH SAUSAGE 1.25
TUNA 1.35
GRILLED CHEESE 85
TOMATO & BACON 1.75
HOT PASTRAMI 1.95
SHRIMP & CHIPS 2.95
FISH SANDWICHES 1.35
FRENCH FRIES 50
JUMBO BURGER 80
CHEESE BURGER 90
CHILI BURGER 90
CORN ON THE COB 60
PIZZA SLICE 60
WITH SAUSAGE or PEPPERONI 70
COCKY-MOON
FROM CONEY ISLAND
FALAFIL 1.15
TACOS 60
TAQUITOS 60
BURRITO 60
TAMALES with CHILI 1.10
TAMALES & BEANS 95
ICE COLD MILK ½ PINT 30
HOT CHOCOLATE 30 - 50
SALT WATER TAFFY 50
COTTON CANDY 40
POP CORN 40
CANDY APPLE 40
DO NUTS 25 - 30 - 40
COFFEE OR TEA 25
FROZEN BANANA 45
SOFT DRINKS
COLA
DR. PEPPER
HIRES ROOT BEER
PEPSI
PEPSI-DIET
MOUNTAIN DEW
7-UP
FRUIT PUNCH
LEMONADE
ALL DRINKS
25
35
45
65
ORANGE JUICE WILLIE 45-65-90
Specials
ALL DRINKS
Lemonade
COCKY-MOON
TRASH

The pier's centrally located Fun Zone offered a wide variety of midway games for patrons using all types of transportation, including roller skates.

Patrons could try their skills at games including tic-tac-toe, the ring toss, and the balloon water race, hoping to take home prizes.

Restaurants and retail fared better than the former bowling and billiards operation in the hall next to the Hippodrome.

Santa Monica Pier has been a part of my every day for most of my life. It's always been there for me, like a dear old friend. When I came to America from Austria, I settled in Santa Monica because it was the home of the original Muscle Beach, the birthplace of the fitness movement. And next to that location was the Santa Monica Pier. Those photos of me in my youth, with my long hair and the mysterious dark background? Those were taken next to the pier, and that dark background is the underside of the pier. In so many ways, that time and that place were perfect.

Since then, the pier and I have been connected. Even before the days of the amusement park and the pier becoming so popular, I would walk on the pier regularly and watch and learn from people. The pier drew all kinds of people back then, just like it continues to do today.

It is one of the world's great gathering places. Anyone can go there, and anyone can enjoy it! It is a landmark and a destination, but more than that, it is a symbol of California and its incredible lifestyle. When you see a photo of the Santa Monica Pier, you immediately think of California...of America.

I still ride my bicycle by the pier today, sometimes even upon its deck boards, and sometimes I take the time to enjoy a walk on the pier. What I find fascinating and enriching, as I breathe the fresh ocean air and take in the California sunshine, is the pier's inviting atmosphere. Everyone is welcome there, and that is very Californian, very American. The Santa Monica Pier is a truly iconic American place.

—Arnold Schwarzenegger

A young Arnold Scharzenegger poses on the beach with the Santa Monica Pier as his backdrop.

Acknowledgments

A funny thing happened after we published the first edition of *Santa Monica Pier*. People came "out of the woodwork" (an intentional deck-board reference), and approached me with Santa Monica Pier stories that I had not heard before and which, of course, were not within that first (but still very thorough!) book. As such, there are some very specific people who inspired this new edition, and I extend my very sincere thanks to:

Judy Abdo, Daniel Alonzo, Toni Basil, Julie Christopher, Andrea Curl, Sunny Davis, Edward DeLand, Harold Dunnigan. Dorothy "Dottie" Hawkins, Caroline Huber, Donna Kail, Noah Justin, Patrick Lennon, Frank Lloyd, Kathy Lo, Craig Lockwood, Esther Lorenz Maire, Stephanie McLean, Judith Meister, Lisa Peterson, Lorna Peterson, Gilbert Rodriguez, Morgan Runyon, Chavela Saffron, Arnold Schwarzenegger, Erick Simmell, Eleanor Moynier Smead, Sinjin Smith, Elaine Jones Stevenson, Linda Sullivan, Randy Trujillo, Tony Verebes, Tom Volk, Craig Wannberg, Cary Weiss, and Tom Zimmerman.

And, of course, my equally sincere thanks again go out to the people who helped make the first edition possible in 2009: Joan Baez, Jose Bacallao, Bob Barber, Larry Barber, Russell Barnard, Cindy Bendat, Charles Beraud, Pete Breceda, Don Camacho, Diana and Carol Cherman, Stan Chambers, Colleen Creedon, Fred Dahlinger, Patricia DeSimone, Tim Dillenbeck, Denise Fast, Drew Feldman, "Chez Jay" Fiondella, Barry A. Fisher, Susan C. Fletcher, Ben Franz-Knight, Dennis Freidman, Keith Goldsmith, Marlene and Joanie Gordon, Nancy Greenstein, Tony Haig, Tom Hayden, Jim Hernage, Rick Howard, Herb Katz, Jay Kennedy, Katharine King, Jeff Klocke, Mike Lopez, Ernest Marquez, Harry Medved, Brian and Eleanor Morgan, Bob Morris, Maynard and Sheila Ostrow, David Pann, Randi Parent, Sandra Pettit, Stuart Rapeport, Ed Ries, William Rivera, Adriana Roth, Paul Sand, Santa Monica History Museum, Santa Monica Public Library, "Captain Ron" Schur, J.D. Simpson, Jeffrey Stanton, Dace Taub, Jamie Trinkkeller, Arthur Verge, John "Yosh" and Chris Volaski, Jane, Linda and Kathy Whiting,

Barbara Williams, and all of the crew at Santa Monica Harbor Patrol.

Special thanks go to Robert Redford and Arnold Schwarzenegger for their thoughtful and thought-provoking contributions to the book.

To anyone whose name I may have inadvertently overlooked, I offer my most sincere apologies and also my assurance that their great contribution is not forgotten.

Special thanks go to the Santa Monica Pier Corporation—my employers and my colleagues past and present—for giving me the time and opportunity to dedicate my efforts toward the research and writing of this book. The support and encouragement of both Board and staff have been truly inspiring.

Heartfelt thanks also go to Terri Accomazzo, Paddy Calistro, Scott McAuley, and J. Eric Lynxwiler of Angel City Press, whose editorial and artistic expertise made this book even better than I could have imagined.

Finally, I wish to thank my parents, John and Bonnie Harris, as well as my wife, Amanda, and my daughters Hayley, Sadie, and Stella for their understanding and patience with the numerous hours that they lost me to—as Amanda calls the pier—my "other wife."

Joan Jett and Sandy West, of the band The Runaways, enjoy some fries at the Cocky Moon restaurant on the pier, 1977.

About the Author

James Harris is a multi-talented executive and producer with a background in event concepts and management, facility/venue rentals, and non-profit management. He is the official Santa Monica Pier historian, as well as the Executive Director of the Santa Monica Pier Corporation. The Santa Monica Pier is his favorite place in the world, and as Executive Director and pier historian he loves to share his knowledge and passion for the pier with the people of Southern California. He is the author of the play *Save the Pier!* and co-wrote the children's book *Stella Rose and the Sea Dragon* alongside his daughter, Stella. James lives in Santa Monica.

SANTA MONICA PIER: AMERICA'S LAST GREAT PLEASURE PIER

by James Harris, Copyright © 2024 James Harris

Design by J. Eric Lynxwiler, Signpost

10 9 8 7 6 5 4 3 2 1

ISBN-13 978-1-62640-129-7

Library of Congress Cataloging-in-Publication Data is available.

Published by Angel City Press at the Los Angeles Public Library

www.angelcitypress.com • Printed in Canada

IMAGE CREDITS

The images in this book are courtesy of the Santa Monica Pier Corporation, except as listed below: **Academy of Motion Picture Arts and Science, Margaret Herrick Library**: 94, bottom left and bottom right; 95, top left • **Arthur Verge Collection**: 57, top; 78 • **Barber, Larry**: 153, center • **Bauer, Bill**: 90; 96; 141; 174 • **Bilous, Jon**: 2 • **Brittain, Tom**: 106, endsheets • **Cincola Family**, the family of Michele "Mike" Cincola: 8; 14; 28; 33–38; 40; 42; 44; 130, left and right; 150; 151; 155 • **City of Santa Monica Office of Emergency Management**: 120, left • **Creedon, Collene**: 82; 87, right; 89, top; 136 • **Davis, Sonny**: 145; 156, right • **DeSimone, Patricia**: 118, left; 140, top left; 140, top right • **Dorothy Hawkins Collection**: 61; 70, top; 70, center; 71, top right • **Dunnigan, Harold**: 104 • **Erickson, Leo**: 27; 115; 116; 121 • **Fremon, Keith**: 172 • **Garber, Helen**: 114, right • **Genser, Ken**: 32, right • **Genser, Roger**: 63; 138 • **Gruber, Frank**: 120, right • **Harris, James**: 16; 124; 131 • **Hartouni, Lisa**: 103 • **Hernage, Jim**: 126; 156, left; 156, center; 157 • **Hiles, Sonny**: 11 • **Hulton Archive/Getty Images**: 173 • **The Huntington Library, Ernest Marquez Collection**: 66 • **Jane Whiting Family**: 76, left; 100, top left and top center; 149, right; 164, bottom • **King Features Syndicate**: 77, bottom • **Kinney, Brian**: 4 • **Lacket, Tom**: 107, bottom; 118, right; 119, right; 129; 133 • **Lawson Desrochers Collection**: 50; 78 • **LeJune, Matthew**: 6 • **Los Angeles Public Library, Security National Bank Photo Collection**: 43; 46; 47; 60; 143; and **Los Angeles Herald Examiner Collection**: 148 • **Northrup, Cindy**: 140, bottom • **Reis, Ed**: 77, top • **Rishe, Viviana**: 176 • **Runyon, Morgan**: 135 • **Santa Monica Harbor Patrol**: 55; 56; 73, left; 125; 144, center; 149, left; 162, left • **Santa Monica History Museum**: 12; 18, left; 19, left and right; 20; 22; 23; 48; 49; 53; 57, bottom; 58; 70, bottom; 84; 88; 93; 94, top; 99; 137, left and right; 147, left; 159 • **Santa Monica Public Library**: 18, right; 54, left and right; 64; 67; 69; 80; 86; 92; 98; 101; 108; 152; 153; 153, bottom • **Smead, Eleanor Moynier**: 70, center; 163, center and left • **Tom Zimmerman**: 158 • **UCLA Charles E. Young Research Library Department of Special Collections, Adelbert Bartlett papers**: 30; and • **Los Angeles Daily News Negatives**: 68; 72 • **UCLA Department of Geography, Benjamin and Gladys Thomas Air Photo Archives, Spence Collection**: 62 • **Venti Views**: 166, top • **Vinetz, Tom**: 110; 139; 165; 166, center top, center bottom, and bottom; 167; 170; 168, top left, top center, bottom left, and bottom center; 169, top and bottom • **Wannberg, Craig**: 71, top left; 71, bottom.

"Save the Pier" from *Burning in Water, Drowning in Flame* by Charles Bukowski. © 1963-1968, 1974 Charles Bukowski. Used by permission of HarperCollins Publishers.

"Moby's Dock"